MW01608075

And whatever you do, in word or deed,
do everything in the name of the Lord Jesus,
giving thanks to God the Father through him.
COLOSSIANS 3:17

OUR SHAPING VIRTUES

OCTOBER 2022

ISSUE 5

Editorial

Editor-in-Chief .... Mark Prater

Executive Editor .... Jeff Purswell

General Editors .... Jared Mellinger, Rob Flood

Design & Layout .... Ruth Feldman

Sovereign Grace Churches © 2022

sovereigngrace.com

SOVEREIGN GRACE CHURCHES

TABLE OF CONTENTS

Recommended Reading

INTRODUCTION

Mark Prater

Executive Director, Sovereign Grace Churches (Glen Mills, PA)

W hat do people experience when they walk into a Sovereign Grace church for the first time? Of course, we want them to receive a warm welcome. Even more, we hope they see and experience the fruit of the gospel at work in our lives. To say it another way, gospel-centrality produces a gospel culture that is marked by certain qualities like humility, joy, gratitude, encouragement, generosity, servanthood, and godliness. It's those seven qualities that we call "Shaping Virtues" in Sovereign Grace. We pray that they mark all of our churches regardless of culture, ethnicity, or nation.

This fifth edition of the Sovereign Grace Journal is dedicated to our seven Shaping Virtues. These virtues aren't unique to Sovereign Grace. They will be seen in any church that is committed to keeping the gospel central. For our family of churches, it's our desire that God would use this edition of the Journal to strengthen these virtues in each of our lives and in every Sovereign Grace church. In fact, as I read each article I was both inspired and convicted. I was inspired to grow in each of the seven virtues, and convicted in areas where I am falling short, which only revealed my need for the grace of God that is mine in the gospel.

Mickey Connolly's opening article provides a pithy yet wonderful overview of each of our seven Shaping Virtues. Next you will find seven articles that are more of a deep dive into each virtue, written in a way that will inspire and challenge you to grow by the grace of God. Keep in mind that as the gospel transforms us these virtues will not only be seen in us individually, but also in our homes and in the community of the local church. Therefore, don't miss Andy Farmer's article about how our Shaping Virtues are experienced in small groups and Aaron Mayfield's contribution for how these virtues are important in building a gospel-centered home. And make sure to peruse the book recommendations which will point you to resources that will help you grow as you apply the gospel to your life. We have carefully selected one book to recommend for each of the Shaping Virtues.

We publish the Sovereign Grace Journal with the hope that it will influence generations to come. I dream of a day, long after I'm gone and in glory, when someone reads this edition of the Journal and knows what it means to be in a Sovereign Grace church. May the power of the gospel produce that kind of gospel heritage, and may the power of the gospel produce that kind of gospel fruit found in the Shaping Virtues for generations to come, all for the glory of God.

Mark

1

THE SHAPING VIRTUES OF SOVEREIGN GRACE CHURCHES

Mickey Connolly

Elder, Crossway Community Church (Charlotte, NC)

W hen the gospel of Jesus Christ is embraced, it produces a culture marked by the fruit of the gospel. All churches that have come to know the grace of God should prioritize and pursue those qualities that are in keeping with the message of grace. In Sovereign Grace, the explicit gospel-focus that has marked our history has led us to value seven particular Shaping Virtues: humility, joy, gratitude, encouragement, generosity, servanthood, and godliness.

Our Shared Values and our Shaping Virtues must work together. Values without virtues will be cold and ultimately unattractive, neither glorifying God nor adorning the gospel. Virtues without values will be shallow because they are untethered to gospel truth.

Although there are specific ways we can cultivate each of these virtues, the primary way we grow in all of them is by immersing ourselves in the message of the death and resurrection of Jesus Christ. Every church member has a vital role to play in promoting a gospel culture by demonstrating these qualities. Pastors in particular must model these virtues in their own lives, setting an example for the flock and helping shape the church.

The following list is not exhaustive. None of us perfectly demonstrates these qualities, and for this reason we press on toward a fuller expression of each Shaping Virtue in our lives. Ultimately, it is God who graciously creates and grows these qualities in his people, and he has promised to bring to completion the good work he began in us. As we labor to keep Christ central in Sovereign Grace, our hope and prayer is that these Shaping Virtues will be present and increase in our churches for generations to come.

Humility

The Lord promises to bless the one "who is humble and contrite in spirit" (Isa. 66:2). Humility is foundational to all our other Shaping Virtues, because without humility we will experience neither the desire nor the grace necessary to cultivate them. The great enemy of all these virtues is pride. Their greatest friend is humility. Jerry Bridges said, "Humility opens the way to all other godly character traits. It is the soil in which the other traits of the fruit of the Spirit grow."[1]

---

[1] Jerry Bridges, *The Fruitful Life* (Colorado Springs, CO: NavPress, 2006), 49.

Humility comes from "honestly assessing ourselves in light of God's holiness and our sinfulness."[2] When we encounter the gospel of Christ, we are humbled as we recognize that, as sinners, our salvation isn't merited in any way but is given freely by grace and grace alone—"by grace you have been saved through faith. And this is not your own doing; it is the gift of God, not a result of works, so that no one may boast" (Eph. 2:8–9). The gospel continues to humble us as we increasingly recognize that the only way we both relate to and receive from God is grace, and not anything we do or don't do.

The message of grace also humbles us in relation to one another, lowering our view of our own importance and raising our view of others. We are consistently exhorted to this humility in Scripture: "I therefore...urge you to walk in a manner worthy of the calling to which you have been called, with all humility" (Eph. 4:1–2); "Put on then, as God's chosen ones...humility" (Col. 3:12); "Humble yourselves before the Lord (Jas. 4:10); "Clothe yourself, all of you, with humility toward one another" (1 Pet. 5:5). Note that humility isn't simply a way we feel but a way we act toward others. It includes inviting and pursuing correction from others.

Finally, the gospel provides both the model and the motive for considering others better than ourselves. Paul's exhortation to "Do nothing from selfish ambition or conceit, but in humility count others more significant than yourselves" and to "look not only to his own interests, but also to the interests of others" (Phil. 2:3–4) is rooted in Jesus' stunning example of humility in

---

[2] C.J. Mahaney, *Humility: True Greatness* (Sisters, OR: Multnomah, 2005), 22.

Philippians 2:5–8. Humility like this creates fertile soil for all the other virtues to flourish, as our eyes look away from ourselves and are fixed on Christ.

Joy

In Philippians 4:4, Paul exhorts believers to "Rejoice in the Lord always." But how are we to do that when life in a fallen world is often full of difficulties, disappointments, and suffering? The answer lies in the reality that in the gospel, we have a source of joy that cannot be touched by any circumstance in this life, no matter how bad.

The gospel is "good news of great joy...for all the people" (Luke 2:10). As believers hear and embrace the good news of salvation by grace alone, the natural response is to rejoice. Our greatest trouble in life has been dealt with once and for all. We are "justified by his grace as a gift" (Rom. 3:24), forgiven of all our sins, and forever reconciled to him. And that's just the start.

We are adopted as sons and daughters into God's family. We are given the Holy Spirit to empower our daily walk with him, and that same Spirit is the "guarantee of our inheritance until we acquire possession of it" (Eph. 1:14). Our inheritance is eternal life in the new heavens and earth where "He will wipe away every tear from their eyes, and death shall be no more, neither shall there be mourning, nor crying, nor pain anymore, for the former things have passed away" (Rev. 21:4). And even more gloriously, we shall "see his face" (Rev. 22:4), as the apex of God's redemptive plan. It is no wonder that Peter can say, "Though you have not seen him, you love him. Though you do not now see him, you believe in him and rejoice with joy that is inexpressible and filled with glory" (1 Pet. 1:8). We, of all people, have reason for joy!

But what about our suffering? Scripture doesn't pretend that life is easy. It honestly admits to the reality of crying, mourning, and pain. But it also helps us to understand that even those moments are tempered by this untouchable joy, because we know that God has ordained them for our good. That's why we can "Count it all joy…when you meet trials of various kinds" (Jas. 1:2) and actually "rejoice in our sufferings" (Rom. 5:3). We rejoice not just because some day we will escape this world and all suffering will end, but because our suffering now is actually "preparing for us an eternal weight of glory beyond all comparison" (2 Cor. 4:17).

Repeatedly preaching the gospel to ourselves positions us for this kind of joy, even in suffering. Ultimately, though, the Holy Spirit produces this joy by his indwelling presence (Gal. 5:22). Gospel joy is contagious joy, and joyful believers will produce joyful churches and joyful gatherings.

Gratitude

The manifold blessings of the gospel are ours as a free and undeserved gift from our gracious God. The only appropriate response to such generous grace is gratitude. "I give thanks to you, O Lord my God, with my whole heart" (Ps. 86:12). A thankful heart is cultivated as we remember, understand, and appreciate the many benefits of the gospel.

We receive many graces as children of God: forgiveness, adoption, our helper the Holy Spirit, the Word illuminated, the privilege of prayer, the church, spiritual gifts for the common good, and divine promises for wisdom and guidance. This list could go on and on, since we are appropriately to be "giving thanks always and for everything to God the Father in the name of our Lord Jesus Christ" (Eph. 5:20). In all of this, God guards and protects us by giving grace in the face of temptation and spiritual armor to be able to stand against the schemes of the devil.

These gospel benefits are more than enough to fill our hearts with thankfulness. Yet God has also provided blessings through his common grace. "In him we live and move and have our being" (Acts 17:28). God has created a world that is beautiful and awe inspiring. The heavens declare his glory and the earth is full of his glory. He feeds, clothes, and shelters us, and he blesses many of us well beyond the mere necessities of life. Paul sums it up in 1 Timothy 6:17 when he speaks of "God, who richly provides us with everything to enjoy." And then there are the people in our lives that have been a blessing: parents, siblings, spouse, children, friends, teachers, and others.

We are especially grateful for other Christians in the local church to which God has joined us. Paul's example of thanksgiving for others is compelling. In his letters to various churches he constantly expresses his gratitude for God's people: "We give thanks to God always for all of you" (1 Thess. 1:2). Each local church, therefore, is to be a community of gratitude, giving thanks to God in everything we do: "And whatever you do, in word or deed, do everything in the name of the Lord Jesus, giving thanks to God the Father through him" (Col. 3:17).

Encouragement

To encourage means to give support, confidence, or hope. God delights to strengthen and sustain his people through the ministry of encouragement. There is nothing more encouraging to our souls than knowing that because of Christ, we are and will always remain in right standing with God. Encouragement is designed by God to build faith and impart grace to keep us going in our Christian walk. Because we live in a fallen world, and because even as believers we can grow discouraged and weary as we serve, suffer, and battle remaining sin, encouragement is a daily necessity.

Effective encouragement focuses on who God is, what he has done for us in Christ, and his promises of ongoing work in our lives. These truths include God's fatherly affection and care for his children, his steadfast love, persistent grace, everlasting mercy, enduring patience, sovereign power, and infinite wisdom. It includes his promises to work all things together for our good (Rom. 8:28), that his grace is sufficient for you (2 Cor. 12:9), and that in all the ups and downs of life he "will never leave you nor forsake you" (Heb. 13:5). Jude assures us that he is able "to keep you from stumbling and present you blameless before the presence of his glory with great joy" (Jude 24). We can "hold fast the confession of our hope without wavering, for he who promised is faithful" (Heb. 10:23). It is no wonder that Paul calls him "the God of endurance and encouragement" (Rom. 15:5)!

Although every believer can and must encourage themselves in the Lord, the emphasis in Scripture falls on the privilege, joy, and responsibility we have to discover evidences of grace in others and remind each other of the truth. In Paul's visits and letters, he regularly encouraged the recipients by reminding them of God's character and promises and by pointing out his grace in their lives. Paul and Barnabas strengthened "the souls of the disciples, encouraging them to continue in the faith" (Acts 14:22).

Every believer is exhorted to "encourage one another and build one another up" (1 Thess. 5:11). We are to "exhort one another every day, as long as it is called 'today,' that none of you may be hardened by the deceitfulness of sin" (Heb. 3:13).

> Consider how to stir up one another to love and good works, not neglecting to meet together, as is the habit of some, but encouraging one another, and all the more as you see the Day drawing near (Heb. 10:24–25).

Note that we are to proactively "consider" how to make this happen. Effective encouragers perceive other's graces and needs, whether big and small, and are prepared to speak edifying words when opportunities arise.

Generosity

The gospel of Jesus Christ is an act of cosmic generosity on God's part, revealing the riches of his love, grace, and mercy. In the gospel we see the overflow of God's love: "God so loved the world that he gave his only Son, that whoever believes in him should not perish but have eternal life" (John 3:16). We also see the overflow of God's grace: "For [we] know the grace of our Lord Jesus Christ, that though he was rich yet for your sake he became poor, so that you by his poverty might become rich" (2 Cor. 8:9). And, we see the overflow of God's mercy: "But God being rich in mercy, because of the great love with which he loved us, even when we were dead in our trespasses, made us alive together with Christ" (Eph. 2:4–5). God didn't just barely save us. The gospel's provision is rich and abundant and complete in every way.

All things belong to God, the giver of every good and perfect gift (Jas. 1:17). Thankfully, God is a generous owner. In Christ, he continues to generously and abundantly bless us. Paul, helps us understand the fullness of the gospel's blessings when he asks, "He who did not spare his own Son but gave him up for us all, how will he not also with him graciously give us all things?" (Rom. 8:32) If God gave us what is most precious to Him—"his own Son"—there is nothing, either material or spiritual that we have need of, that he would now withhold. Truly, Jesus came that we "may have life and have it abundantly" (John 10:10).

When our hearts are transformed by the gospel, God's own generosity is unleashed in our lives. God has extravagantly blessed us, and now we delight in blessing others, using our time, energy, and resources for their good. We taste of the reality that "it is more blessed to give than to receive" (Acts 20:35). We view our own blessings not as indulgent gifts, but as opportunities to bless others and "produce thanksgiving to God" (2 Cor. 9:11).

The gospel also creates a heavenly-mindedness in us that frees us from greed and covetousness in this world to invest in the world to come, because there we have "an inheritance that is imperishable, undefiled, and unfading, kept in heaven for you" (1 Pet. 1:4). We can now generously and cheerfully "lay up...treasures in heaven" by using our time, talent, and money for his kingdom (Matt. 6:20).

Servanthood

The gospel saves us into a life of service, first to God and then to others as an expression of that service. "For what we proclaim is not ourselves, but Jesus Christ as Lord, with ourselves as your servants for Jesus' sake" (2 Cor. 4:5). If humility is the foundation of our shaping virtues, servanthood is their concrete expression. The humble, joyful, grateful, encouraging, generous, loving believer simply can't help but have those virtues overflow in a life of practical service.

Jesus left us with a clear example of this life of service that is at the heart of our gospel calling. As his disciples argued among themselves about who was the greatest, Jesus redefined true greatness:

> You know that those who are considered rulers of the Gentiles lord it over them, and their great ones exercise authority over them. But it shall not be so among you. But whoever would be great among you must be your servant, and whoever would be first among you must be slave of all (Mark 10:42–44).

And to emphasize the point, he made this stunning statement: "For even the Son of Man came not to be served but to serve, and to give his life as a ransom for many" (Mark 10:45).

The death of Christ is the greatest demonstration of that service, but not the only one. To show exactly what such service should look like, Jesus washed his disciples' feet, fully cognizant of his divinity and of the looming cross. He explained,

> You call me Teacher and Lord, and you are right, for so I am. If I then, your Lord and Teacher, have washed your feet, you also ought to wash one another's feet. For I have given you an example, that you also should do just as I have done to you (John 13:13–15).

Indeed, it was Christ's coming death, which would truly "wash" the disciples, that was to serve as their deepest motivation in serving others

Thus, we care for one another in the context of local church communities. This is not only an intent of the gospel, it is also one of the fruits of the gospel. God's love has been placed in our hearts, enabling Christians to love in ordinary and extraordinary ways. In I John this connection is explained:

> Beloved, let us love one another, for love is from God, and whoever loves has been born of God and knows God. Anyone who does not love does not know God, because God is love...Beloved, if God so loved us, we also ought to love one another (1 John 4:7–8, 11).

We are given the necessary grace to live this way. Paul explains that "To each is given the manifestation of the Spirit for the common good" (1 Cor. 12:7). Peter emphasizes the purpose of such gifts: "As each has received a gift, use it to serve one another, as good stewards of God's varied grace" (1 Pet. 4:10). In the parable of the talents in Matthew 25, Jesus emphasizes our responsibility to use the gifts and graces God has given us, but also teaches the heavenly reward his servants will receive. "Well done, good and faithful servant" (Matt. 25:23) is the commendation every believer longs to hear on that day.

Godliness

Justification means that God has declared guilty sinners to be righteous through faith in the life, death, and resurrection of Jesus. This justification is "by his grace as a gift" (Rom. 3:24) and, once given, can't be lost or taken away because it rests on Jesus' finished work and not our ongoing performance. Thus, those who are freely saved through the gospel are also called, empowered, and motivated to please the one who saved them.

Justified believers are called to "let your manner of life be worthy of the gospel" (Phil. 1:27), to "strive for...the holiness without which no one will see the Lord (Heb. 12:14), and to "cleanse ourselves from every defilement of body and spirit, bringing holiness to completion in the fear of God" (2 Cor. 7:1). All these passages refer to the call to progressive sanctification: a process in which one's moral condition is increasingly brought into conformity with one's justified status before God.

Like justification, sanctification is a work of grace. Many make the mistake of thinking that we are saved by grace, but that we then become holy by our own efforts. This is simply not true. We are justified by grace and we are sanctified by grace as well. The difference, however, is that in justification God alone works, but in sanctification we are active participants with the Holy Spirit in receiving and responding to God's grace to us.

The problem for many Christians comes when we confuse these two aspects of God's work in our lives. This confusion can lead either to license—believing it doesn't matter how we live since we are justified—or legalism, which is living as if relating to God is on the basis of our performance rather than by faith in the performance of Christ.

Philippians 2:12–13 is key to understanding God's role and ours in our growth. Paul writes, "work out your own salvation with fear and trembling, for it is God who works in you, both to will and to work for his good pleasure." We work out our salvation by putting sin to death and by putting on godly virtues. God the Holy Spirit works by enabling us to "will" (the desire for godliness) and to "work" (efforts toward godliness) in the process of becoming more like Christ. It is the Spirit who empowers our battles against temptation and sin and produces spiritual fruit in our lives (Gal. 5:17, 22–23).

Motivated by a desire to please and honor the Lord, Christians are to strive after holiness (Heb. 12:14) and be doers of the word (Jas. 1:22). We put sin to death (Col. 3:5) and we live in all things for God (Col. 3:17). In so doing, our lives testify to the goodness of

God, the power of the Holy Spirit, and the reality of the gospel. We pursue godliness in the confidence of knowing that God will sanctify us completely at the coming of our Lord Jesus Christ (1 Thess. 5:23). "He who calls you is faithful; he will surely do it" (1 Thess. 5:24).

Cultivating These Virtues

Humility, joy, gratitude, encouragement, generosity, servanthood, and godliness. These are the Shaping Virtues that the gospel creates and that God calls us to continually pursue. They are qualities we have valued throughout our history in Sovereign Grace, and ones that ought to increasingly mark our life together in our churches as we press on to maturity.

We would do well to ask ourselves, "Am I shaped by these virtues? Where do I need to grow?" Pastors would be wise to assess whether the culture of the church they serve is shaped by these virtues, and how to grow through teaching and example. The joyous news is that we already possess the key to such growth: the glorious gospel of Jesus Christ, with all the transforming power it brings into our lives. By God's grace, let's continue to pray for, prioritize, and pursue these shaping virtues in Sovereign Grace churches, for the glory of Christ and the advance of the gospel.

2

HUMILITY

PURSUING TRUE GREATNESS

C. J. Mahaney

Senior Pastor, Sovereign Grace Church (Louisville, KY)

F rom[3] the earliest days of Sovereign Grace Churches, there has been an emphasis placed upon the priority and pursuit of humility. This is not an emphasis unique to us or something we came up with, but an emphasis that God holds out for his people in Holy Scripture.

In Isaiah 66:1–2, we encounter these remarkable words:

> Thus says the LORD: "Heaven is my throne, and the earth is my footstool; what is the house that you would build for me, and what is the place of my rest? All these things my hand has made, and so all these things came to be, declares the LORD. But this is the one to whom I will look: he who is humble and contrite in spirit and trembles at my word.

---

[3] A version of this article first appeared in Thomas K. Ascol, ed., *Dear Timothy: Letters on Pastoral Ministry* (Cape Coral, FL: Founders Press, 2004). Used with Permission.

The Israelites had a lot going for them. They had a unique identity. They had the Torah. They had the Law of God, the Covenant, and the temple. But they lacked humility—they had allowed pride to flourish unchecked. So God draws their attention away from the temple and toward their hearts. He tells them that their preoccupation ought not to be with the grandeur of externals, but with the internal. "This is the one to whom I will look: he who is humble and contrite in spirit and trembles at my word" (Isa. 66:2).

The Perils of Pride

Due to remaining sin, all of us are prone to pride. I do not consider myself a humble person, rather, I am a proud person pursuing humility by the grace of God. We must be aware of our pride, and we must be aware of the perils of pride. Pastors in particular must be aware that, as ministers of the gospel, pride has the potential in our lives to leverage itself through ministry, doing damage that extends far beyond our own families.

John Stott wrote this about pride: "At every stage of our Christian development and in every sphere of our Christian discipleship, pride is our greatest enemy and humility our greatest friend."[4] As best I can tell, pride was the first sin—among angels and among men. And it would appear that pride is the essence of all sin, as well as the sin God finds most offensive. The proud man heads up the list of God's seven hated abominations in Proverbs 6. When referring to pride, the Bible uses words like hate, abomination, and detestable. Stronger language is simply not available.

---

[4] J.I. Packer & Loren Wilkinson, eds. *Alive to God* (Downers Grove, IL: InterVarsity Press, 1992), 119.

Besides the things I "hate" in the humorous sense—things like cottage cheese and professional sports teams from New York—I do in all seriousness genuinely hate sin and evil, and the damage sin does in the world. But set my hatred side by side with the supremely pure, holy, and unalterable hatred that God has for the sin of pride, and they will appear as nothing but casual disinclinations. We simply cannot overstate how deeply God detests and abhors pride.

Why does God so hate pride? Charles Bridges summed it up well, "Pride lifts up the heart against God. It contends for the supremacy with him."[5] Pride is an attitude of self-sufficiency and independence toward God and of self-righteousness and superiority toward others. It robs God of the honor and glory due him. It takes many forms but has only one goal: self-glorification. No wonder then that God opposes the proud (1 Pet. 5:5).

Oh, the perils of pride! I've seen it ruin pastors, marriages, families, relationships, churches—all this among sincere believers. But for all the very real perils of pride, there is also the rich promise of humility. For our God is not only passionately opposed to pride; he is decisively drawn to humility. The omniscient One is aware of all things—nothing escapes his notice—yet he actively searches for one thing. His attention is uniquely drawn to humility: "This is the one to whom I will look." The humble man will receive grace, and not opposition, because his motive is to glorify God, not himself. God will always support and extend favor to a humble man who pursues God's will.

---

[5] Charles Bridges, *The Commentary on Proverbs* (reprint, Carlisle, PA: The Banner of Truth Trust, 1968), 228.

The Application of Truth

Imagine a number of churches, each one led by called, gifted, and committed pastors. Each one holding a high view of Scripture and of sound doctrine. Each one devoted to the centrality of the gospel and filled with committed, servant-hearted believers who love the Lord Jesus in sincerity. Over time, some of these churches thrive, but some do not. Why is that? At the risk of oversimplifying, I think I know the answer.

Many people, of course, believe the Bible. Many pastors know it extremely well. Many recognize that it is our only truly reliable guide for life and faith. But strong churches—that is, churches in which the members are growing in sanctification and increasingly glorifying God in their public and private lives—are churches in which the pastors do not merely teach sound doctrine. They also lead in and model the consistent application of biblical truth to all of life.

So this I can say with full confidence: over the decades, a pastor's ministry will be fruitful only to the extent that we have both taught Scripture accurately and applied it consistently to ourselves, our families, our fellow elders, and the churches we serve. It is not biblical truth alone that builds effective churches. It is, by God's grace, the application of biblical truth.

The proper application of Scripture will always emphasize the weakening of pride (our greatest enemy) and the cultivation of humility (our greatest friend). I'm convinced this will make a huge difference in our churches.

How to Cultivate Humility

Christians have a desire to tremble at God's Word. Surely this phrase speaks of something far beyond mere mental assent. The proud man may respect God's Word, he may believe it, he may teach it, but to tremble before it is a mark of the humble. So, what practical steps can Christians take to cultivate humility and thus tremble at God's Word?

The Attributes of God

First, study the attributes of God. Focus especially on God's incommunicable attributes, those having no reflection or illustration in man or indeed anywhere in creation. (Note how, in the Isaiah 66 passage I quoted, God draws our attention to his unique and unparalleled greatness.)

Consider, for example, that God is infinite. He has no boundaries, no edges. He is also omnipresent. He has no center, no one point of concentration, no single place where his essence is located, for he is fully and equally present everywhere—within creation and beyond it. *New Bible Dictionary* says, "When we say that God is infinite spirit, we pass completely out of the reach of our experience."[6]

Truly, this is the deep end of the theological pool. This infinite One is self-existent and self-sufficient. Everything in creation, from you and me, to the heavenly beings, to the atoms of gas in deepest space, is in complete dependence on God's sustaining attention for mere moment-by-moment existence. But before

---

[6] J.D. Douglas, et al., (eds.), *New Bible Dictionary* (Wheaton, IL: Tyndale House Publishers Inc., 1962), 427.

time, through all of time, and outside of time, God depends ever and only upon himself. We are like the grass that withers and fades, but he alone possesses the power of sheer being. As Matthew Henry wrote,

> The greatest and best men in the world must say "By the grace of God I am what I am." But God says absolutely—and it is more than any creature, man or angel, can say—"I am that I am."[7]

Such contemplation will inevitably weaken our pride. The greater our awareness of the difference between ourselves and God, the more we will experience and express humility. How good of God to offer us in his Word a glimpse of his unfathomable other-ness, that we might have it as an unerring aid to humility!

Stay Near the Cross

Second, never stray from the cross. Live as one who continually surveys—and from close range—the wondrous cross on which the Prince of Glory died. I can do no more, and I can surely do no better, than to draw your attention to the centrality of our Savior's sacrifice.

A friend told me of an opportunity he once had to interview Carl Henry, a truly humble man who is perhaps the foremost evangelical scholar of the latter half of the twentieth century. He asked Dr. Henry, then in his late seventies, how he had remained so humble for so many decades. Dr. Henry replied, "How can

---

[7] Matthew Henry, *Commentary on the Whole Bible,* vol. 1 (Old Tappan, NJ: Fleming H. Revell Company, n.d.), 284 [Exodus 3:14].

anyone be arrogant when he stands beside the cross?" In his book *The Cross of Christ*, John Stott says, "The cross does not flatter us, the cross undermines our self-righteousness. We can stand before it only with a bowed head and a broken spirit."[8]

The Doctrines of Grace

Third, study the doctrines of grace. As you immerse yourself in the study of election, calling, justification, and perseverance, you will be reminded that all we have and all we are as Christians begins with God, ends with God, and depends on God. These rich doctrines leave no room for self-congratulation. Mark Webb writes,

> God intentionally designed salvation so that no man can boast of it. He didn't merely arrange it so that boasting would be discouraged or kept to a minimum. He planned it so that boasting would be absolutely excluded. Election does precisely that.[9]

Personal arrogance and a true appreciation of reformation theology cannot long co-exist; truth will drive out the lie of pride.

The Doctrine of Sin

Fourth, study the doctrine of sin. The best way to prepare for a study of sin is first to study God's holiness, for there and there alone do we encounter the complete absence of sin. Search the

---

[8] John Stott, *The Cross of Christ* (Downers Grove, IL: InterVarsity Press, 1986), 12.
[9] Mark Webb, "What Difference Does it Make?" *Reformation & Revival Journal 3*, no. 1 (Winter 1994)

Scriptures thoroughly on the topic, and read R.C. Sproul's *The Holiness of God*. Then, when you begin to study the doctrine of sin itself, you will bring to the task a proper perspective. For your reading here, none can improve upon John Owen, especially *Temptation and Sin* in Volume Six of his collected works. An abridged version is available as a book titled *Sin and Temptation*. Also, Kris Lundgaard's *The Enemy Within* is essentially a simplified and modernized interpretation of Owen's work that is nevertheless quite effective.

As you study the doctrine of sin, be sure to do so in light of the cross of Christ, being careful to apply and celebrate the grace of God. This is crucial, because it is possible to teach this doctrine and not reveal the grace of our Lord Jesus Christ. It takes great skill to teach the doctrine of sin in a way that reveals, rather than obscures, the grace of Christ. Sinclair Ferguson captures this challenge:

> Only by seeing our sin do we come to see the need for and wonder of grace. But exposing sin is not the same thing as unveiling and applying grace. We must be familiar with and exponents of its multifaceted power, and know how to apply it to a variety of spiritual conditions.
>
> Truth to tell, exposing sin is easier than applying grace; for, alas, we are more intimate with the former than we sometimes are with the latter. Therein lies our weakness.[10]

---

[10] Sinclair Ferguson, "A Preacher's Decalogue Part II," Reformation21, (accessed March 27, 2009).

So we must handle the doctrine of sin with great care, and in a manner that shows the stunning magnitude and power of the grace of Christ. But we must not avoid the doctrine of sin—it is of immeasurable value to our churches, and in cultivating humility in our lives.

Confession and Correction

Fifth, we pursue humility by applying the doctrine of sin through confession and inviting correction. Noting that all men are sinners, Mike Renihan further observes, "Sinners fall into two more distinct classes: those who admit their sin and those who don't. Those who admit themselves to be sinners fall into two more classes: those who do something about it and those who do not."[11] The humble Christian is the man or woman who does something about it, especially through confession and the pursuit of correction.

It's not difficult to acknowledge one's pervasive depravity. What's difficult is specifically to confess an area of personal depravity. Obviously, one must first confess sins to God. But we are also called to confess, as appropriate, to individuals.

I feel strongly that every pastor, even in the smallest church, must have a team of men to whom he is accountable. These are men to be transparent with, to whom we confess our sins freely and regularly. Let these confessions be full and specific, not selective and partial. Confess overt acts of sin as well as present temptations, and let grace and forgiveness be abundant. It's a sad truth that whenever a pastor disqualifies himself from ministry through a

---

[11] Mike Reniham, "A Pastor's Pride and Joy." *TableTalk* (July 1999), 53.

failure of personal character, a long-standing lack of confession has invariably been present.

Another vital means of applying the doctrine of sin to our own lives is to invite and pursue correction in areas of character. People in our lives should feel truly welcome to point out to us any instance in which it appears you have behaved sinfully—or indeed, any area in which you could simply be doing a better job. Would your wife, your friends, and those who serve with you in your church say you are easy to entreat?

Again, as we walk in confession and invite correction, we must ensure that we do so in a way that contributes to a culture of grace. Every confession of sin is an opportunity to marvel at the grace of God in the gospel.

Practices to Consider

For years I have had a list of daily practices as I seek to grow in humility. It is a great help in the pursuit of humility to observe some set of concrete, tangible practices. Here are the ones that, by God's grace, have proven effective for me. I'm not encouraging any strict emulation of these. The principle of pursuing humility can be expressed in many ways, and it is important to distinguish biblical principles from individual practices. I offer these practices for your consideration and, I hope, for your provocation. Custom-design your own list. But for the sake of your family and your church, be sure to move from general principles to specific practices.

1. Begin the day acknowledging your dependence upon God, your need for God, and your confidence in God. I'm talking the first thoughts of the day. When that alarm goes off, I'm immediately seeking to direct my heart to God that I might express my dependence on him. I continue purposefully to cultivate this attitude as I prepare for the day. If not, my thoughts will—without fail—drift toward self-reliance.

2. As you turn your thoughts to God, set the tone for the day by expressing gratefulness to him. "Thankfulness is a soil in which pride does not easily grow."[12] And thankfulness begins with the gospel. The best way I have found to battle the forgetfulness and distractions that so easily hinder our gratitude is—as Jerry Bridges says—to preach the gospel to yourself every day. So begin each day doing just that, and then direct your gratitude to God because of the gospel.

As the day progresses, purpose to recognize and express gratitude for the innumerable "Post-It notes" that God places around us to remind us of his grace. It is said of Matthew Henry that to encounter him was to become aware of an alert and thankful observer of answered prayer. I want to be like that. Ingratitude is the mark of a proud man but to consistently express thankfulness is to deal blow after mortifying blow to my self-glorifying arrogance.

3. Practice the spiritual disciplines every day. The spiritual disciplines are a daily declaration and demonstration of my need for God and my dependence on him. I believe that our

---

[12] Michael Ramsey, *The Christian Priest Today* (London: SPCK, 1972), 79.

inconsistency in practicing the spiritual disciplines is not due primarily to an absence of self-discipline, but to the presence of self-sufficiency.

4. Seize your daily commute, if you have one, to memorize and meditate on Scripture. When William Wilberforce was serving in the House of Commons, he used his daily one-mile walk from his home to Parliament to recite from memory the whole of Psalm 119. Now that is time well spent.

5. All day long, at the moment you become aware of burdensome cares, cast them upon the Lord, who cares for you. Where there is worry and anxiety, there is the pride of self-reliance. The humble man, though he may be responsible for many things, is free of care—he is care-free. His life is characterized by joy and peace, for it is impossible to be worried while trusting in the Sovereign One.

6. When my work day concludes, instead of simply leaving for home, I seize the opportunity to cultivate humility. No matter how "successful" or "unsuccessful" my day has been (in my limited estimation), I acknowledge that God is the only One who ever perfectly completes his daily to-do list, and I commit all that remains undone to his safe keeping. Tomorrow, I'll come back and, by his grace, try again.

7. At the end of the day, I seek to transfer all glory to God. Puritan Thomas Watson wrote, "When we have done anything praiseworthy we must hide ourselves under the veil of humility and transfer the glory of all we have done to God."[13] Thankful for such precious advice, I take a few moments in the evening just to mentally review the day. For every evidence of fruitfulness or progress I've witnessed or experienced that day, I try to specifically acknowledge to God the undeniable fact that He alone is responsible.

As a pastor, I may be a means of grace in the lives of others, but I can't save anyone! I can't convict anyone of sin or bring a soul to repentance. I have no power in me to effect sanctification in anyone's life. Our churches are testimonies to the greatness and graciousness of God—not monuments to our leadership and preaching.

On one occasion when Charles Spurgeon was addressing his Pastors College students, he told them, "Your ministry is poor enough. Everybody knows it, and you ought to know it most of all."[14] Now, was he pointing out that this class of students was particularly incompetent? Not at all. He went on to inform them that preaching is ever and only effective because God keeps His promise that His Word shall not return void. Isaiah acknowledged to God, "You have indeed done for us all our works" (Isa. 26:12), and this, as *The Expositor's Bible Commentary* notes, is "a profound truth, blessedly destructive of spiritual pride."[15] God is the prime mover behind every means of grace. Soli Deo Gloria!

---

[13] Thomas Watson, *A Body of Divinity* (Carlisle, PA: The Banner of Truth Trust, 1992), 17.

[14] Charles Spurgeon, *Lectures to My Students* (reprint, Grand Rapids, MI: Zondervan Publishing House, 1981), 194.

[15] Frank E. Gaebelein, ed. *The Expositor's Bible Commentary* (Grand Rapids, MI: Zondervan Publishing House, 1986), 165.

8. Finally, before going to sleep at night, I acknowledge that sleep is a gift from the Creator to the creature. I don't just passively fall asleep. I seize that daily opportunity to weaken pride and cultivate humility by acknowledging him who neither slumbers nor sleeps. Sleep, for me, is a daily reminder that I am far from self-sufficient. Let me put it this way: I have a desperate, irreversible, physiological need to spend a substantial portion of every twenty-four hours in a state of mental and physical incapacity, utterly helpless and completely useless. Is this not comical? God then uses this time to strengthen and restore me for another day—a day in which I will invariably fail to obey him fully, yet by grace he will somehow redeem my actions to produce a measure of fruitfulness. How can this not be humbling?

I pray that these thoughts will inspire you to establish patterns of your own that will serve you for the rest of your life, as these have served me.

Motivated by Grace

So let us devote ourselves daily to the purposeful application of Scripture, that we might avoid the perils of pride and experience the promise of humility. And let us do so motivated by grace. For however intentional our efforts, and however much we might see God's grace at work in sanctification, we do not rest in our accomplishments or good intentions as if they could ever earn us anything before a Holy God. We claim no merit in what we do. Rather, we rest in the finished work of the Savior. We are God's and enjoy his favor only because Another has perfectly fulfilled all the righteous requirements of the law.

Jesus Christ is the only One who has ever been perfectly humble, completely contrite in spirit, and fully observant of what it means to tremble at God's Word. We rest ultimately in him—in his perfect life and substitutionary sacrifice for our sins.

3

JOY
REJOICE IN THE LORD ALWAYS

Jared Mellinger

Senior Pastor, Covenant Fellowship Church (Glen Mills, PA)

S eminary professor and church historian Dr. Scott Manetsch
wrote a book about pastoral ministry in Geneva in the 1500s.
The pastors in Geneva during the time were faithful in many ways,
and yet they were not perfect. One weakness Dr. Manetsch points
out is that some of Geneva's ministers "drew criticism from time to
time for sermons that were too severe or too pointed"[16] and

> several men were particularly notorious for stirring
> popular outrage by their vitriolic and abusive preaching.
> Angry words and incessant scolding too easily
> masqueraded as the reformed virtue of "holy vehemence."[17]

One woman complained that "the ministers become angry when
they show zeal in the pulpit."[18] Another young woman said of her

---

[16] Scott Manetsch, *Calvin's Company of Pastors: Pastoral Care and the
Emerging Reformed Church, 1536–1609* (New York, NY: Oxford University
Press, 2013), 175.
[17] Ibid., 175.
[18] Ibid,. 175.

pastor that "whenever he speaks it seems that he wants to bite people."[19]

Manetsch writes,

> Of all the ministers, Raymond Chauvet was probably most hated. A ferocious preacher, Chauvet seems to have delighted in excoriating the sins and sinners that he encountered both in the church and marketplace. In 1546, for example, Chauvet pronounced from his pulpit a curse on members of his congregation who were leaving the sermon early: 'May evil, plague, war, and famine fall upon you!' he cried. Throughout Geneva, they gave him the nickname Torticol—literally, 'pain in the neck.' ...On a number of different occasions Geneva's magistrates and ministers were forced to reprimand their colleague, admonishing him 'not to be so angry and to use greater moderation' in his sermons and conversation.[20]

The Joy of Jesus

In evident contrast to the angry scolding of Raymond Chauvet, Jesus says that the goal of his teaching is that his joy would be in his followers, and that our joy would be full (John 15:11). The joy of Jesus set him apart from the rabbis and other religious leaders of his day. The Pharisees with all their strictness and rules didn't have a category for him. Jesus is the one anointed with the oil of gladness, the one who came eating and drinking, the one whose glad heart made his face cheerful, the one with a radiant

---

[19] Ibid., 175.
[20] Ibid., 175-176.

disposition, enjoying the company of children, the one who went through life and death with joy fixed in his eyes (though he was the man of sorrows), and the one who had the love of the Father etched on his heart.

Likewise, followers of Christ are to be known for their joy. Randy Alcorn says in his book on happiness,

> In most unbelievers' perceptions, Christianity hasn't brought much joy to the world. As a religion, it's primarily known for its rules, self-righteousness, and intolerance—none of which convey gladness and merriment.[21]

And yet what we see in the book of Acts is that one of the most powerful factors in the spread of the gospel was the evident joy of the early church. Joy matters not only for the sake of our souls but for the sake of our witness.

If I had to put my finger on one quality that has marked my church experience in Sovereign Grace Churches in general and in Covenant Fellowship Church in particular, it would be the presence of joy. I have spent my life around Christians who sing with joy, serve with gladness, cultivate gratitude, talk about what it means to be happy pastors, and celebrate the grace that has rescued us from sin and death.

---

[21] Randy Alcorn, *Happiness* (Carol Stream, IL: Tyndale House Publishers, 2015). 29.

No One Will Take Your Joy

When Jesus spoke to his disciples the night before he died, they were troubled and afraid. Jesus told them that the world would hate them (John 15:19) and that in the world they will have tribulation (John 16:33). Jesus says in John 16:6 that in this moment sorrow has filled their hearts. Yet it is because he knows our frame and cares so greatly for us that he speaks truths to his people for the sake of their joy (John 15:11). Jesus does not call us to die to our joy, rather he is aiming for the fullness of our joy! In John 16:20 he says, "You will be sorrowful, but your sorrow will turn to joy." And in John 16:22 he says, "So also you have sorrow now, but I will see you again, and your hearts will rejoice, and no one will take your joy from you." In John 17:13, he prays to the Father concerning us, "that they may have my joy fulfilled in themselves."

When Jesus says that his joy will be in us and our joy will be full, he is not saying that he will give all of his followers a chipper personality or that he will plaster our faces with superficial smiles. True joy is not rooted in temperament. Nor is Jesus saying that we will have trouble-free lives. Someone once said that Jesus promised his disciples three things: that they would be completely fearless, absurdly happy, and in constant trouble.

How can trouble and happiness exist together? Because true joy is not rooted in life circumstances. Even as we are "grieved by various trials" (1 Pet. 1:6), we "rejoice with joy that is inexpressible and filled with glory" (1 Pet. 1:8). When we are mistreated for Christ, we should join the early disciples and rejoice that we are counted worthy to suffer dishonor for the name (Acts 5:41).

"Count it all joy, my brothers, when you meet trials of various kinds" (Jas. 1:2).

It is not that our circumstances are irrelevant, but that we have the deep satisfaction and joy of knowing that however deep our sorrows, the love of Christ is deeper still. He is with us, he will hold us fast, and he is working in those circumstances in ways we don't understand, for our good and for his glory.

How can we experience the joy of Jesus in our lives, and cultivate gladness in our churches?

1. Know the God of all joy.

God is perfectly and eternally happy in himself—he has more gladness than we can comprehend, having the fellowship of the persons of the Godhead as the source of his eternal joy. 1 Timothy 1:11 describes the gospel as "the gospel of the glory of the blessed God." Psalm 16:11 says, "In his presence there is fullness of joy, and at your right hand are pleasures forevermore."

God delights in his glory. He delights in his creation. He delights in his beloved Son, with whom he is well pleased. And remarkably, he delights in us. "The Lord your God is in your midst, a mighty one who will save; he will rejoice over you with gladness; he will quiet you by his love; he will exult over you with loud singing" (Zeph. 3:17). Our God is the singing God, overflowing with joy and gladness. He is eternally happy in himself and has no need of us for his joy. And yet, he invites us to share in that joy for the sake of his glory. The way we honor God is not by somehow trying to make him happier than he would be without us. That is

37

impossible. The way to honor him is to share in his joy by delighting in him.

2. Remember the good news of great joy.

When Christ was born, the gospel was announced as "good news of great joy" (Luke 2:10). The good news is the message of salvation, the love of Christ in his death and resurrection. And it is a message that is calculated to thrill and satisfy our souls. "Be glad and rejoice, for the Lord has done great things!" (Joel 2:21). "With joy you will draw water from the wells of salvation" (Isa. 12:3). Psalm 34:5 says, "Those who look to him are radiant." And in Psalm 90:14, Moses prays, "Satisfy us in the morning with your steadfast love, that we may rejoice and be glad all our days."

The gospel is a message of indescribable joy, declaring that sinners are loved, forgiven, and accepted by a holy God.

3. Abide in Christ every day.

George Müller, whose life did so much good for others and especially for so many orphans, learned the priority of joy.

> According to my judgment the most important point to be attended to is this: above all things see to it that your souls are happy in the Lord. Other things may press upon you, the Lord's work may even have urgent claims upon your attention, but I deliberately repeat, it is of supreme and paramount importance that you should seek above all things to have your souls truly happy in God Himself! Day by day seek to make this the most important business of your life. This has been my firm and settled condition for

the last five and thirty years. For the first four years after my conversion I knew not its vast importance, but now after much experience I specially commend this point to the notice of my younger brethren and sisters in Christ: the secret of all true effectual service is joy in God, having experimental acquaintance and fellowship with God Himself.[22]

Every day, the greatest danger in the Christian life is losing our joy in Christ. Every day, our greatest need is for our own soul to be happy in God, which is just another way of saying that we must learn to abide in Christ through the Word of God and prayer.

4. Delight in the people of God.

In Psalm 16:3 the psalmist says, "As for the saints in the land, they are the excellent ones in whom is all my delight." John says in 3 John 4 that the Christian's great joy is seeing God's grace at work in fellow believers: "I have no greater joy than to hear that my children are walking in the truth." Study the letters of Paul, and you see him constantly thanking God for people and experiencing joy as a result. "For what thanksgiving can we return to God for you, for all the joy that we feel for your sake before our God?" (1 Thess. 3:9).

Even when sin and weakness abound, we should be more aware of grace, searching out things to celebrate and affirm in others. We

---

[22] George Müller, *A Narrative of Some of the Lord's Dealings with George Müller, Written by Himself* (Muskegon, MI: Dust and Ashes Publications, 2003), 731.

cultivate joy by being able to enjoy and delight in a wide range of people in the church, not just those who are like us.

5. Gather with gladness.

I once heard a pastor tell his church that Easter Sunday was approaching, and that people should "come rowdy." There is a sense in which the greatest contribution we can make to a church is to come rowdy—that is, to bring our own passion for Christ to the gathering of the saints. The psalmist says, "I was glad when they said to me, 'Let us go to the house of the Lord!'" (Ps. 122:1). Nehemiah 12:43 describes the corporate joy of God's redeemed people: "And they offered great sacrifices that day and rejoiced, for God had made them rejoice with great joy; the women and children also rejoiced. And the joy of Jerusalem was heard far away."

In Sovereign Grace Churches, we value the Sunday gathering and we value musical worship. Our gathering cultivates and expresses our joy in the Lord.

6. Serve and lead with joy.

In Deuteronomy 28:4–48, God threatened judgment if his people would not serve him "with joyfulness and gladness of heart." Psalm 100:2 gives the command, "Serve the Lord with gladness." Charles Spurgeon once said, "The best work is done by the happy, joyful workman."[23]

---

[23] Charles Spurgeon. March 25, 1888. "Our Great Shepherd Finding the Sheep." Sermon preached at Metropolitan Tabernacle.

One of the verses that has had the greatest influence on my service in pastoral ministry is Hebrews 13:17. Speaking of the pastoral work of keeping watch over souls, it says "Let [pastors] do this with joy and not with groaning, for that would be no advantage to you." The greater a pastor's joy in serving, the more those we serve will benefit from that ministry. Effective preaching and pastoral leadership will convey and reflect the gracious, happy heart of the Father.

A lot of preachers and those who lead in public would do well to smile more in public. Having a joy-filled, radiant countenance as pastors, especially in our preaching, is important because unbelievers often see Christianity as a dreary faith, and believers often assume the heart of their Father toward them is stern. A glad ministry of grace counters the enemy's lies by embodying the truth. Preaching is the primary means for cultivating a culture of joy in the church.

7. Encourage a joy-filled ministry diet.

The ministry we take in and the ministry we extend to others should contribute to a culture of joy. So much of social media works against the cultivation of joy due to the prevalence of criticism, complaining, slander, and outrage. But Christians can promote joy in their own soul and in others by talking more about grace than sin, focusing more on truth than countering falsehood, expressing honor more than criticism, emphasizing what we are for more than what we are against, and living a life marked more by celebration than lamentation.

8. Hope in the return of Christ.

The day is coming when our blessed hope will be realized and Christ will appear to make all things new. God will dwell with his people forever.

> He will wipe away every tear from their eyes, and death shall be no more, neither shall there be mourning, nor crying, nor pain anymore, for the former things have passed away (Rev. 21:4).

 Christians know the end of the story! The bright tomorrow will soon be here!

Therefore, "set your hope fully on the grace that will be brought to you at the revelation of Jesus Christ" (1 Pet. 1:13). And until that day, resolve to work for your own joy and the joy of others, contributing to a culture of gladness in the church.

Deep and Lasting Joy

Octavius Winslow says,

> The religion of Christ is the religion of joy. Christ came to take away our sins, to roll off our curse, to unbind our chains, to open our prison house, to cancel our debt; in a word, to give us the oil of joy for mourning, the garment of praise for the spirit of heaviness. Is not this joy? Where can we find a joy so real, so deep, so pure, so lasting? There is every element of joy—deep, ecstatic, satisfying, sanctifying joy—in the gospel of Christ. The believer in Jesus is essentially a happy man. The child of God is, from

necessity, a joyful man. His sins are forgiven, his soul is justified, his person is adopted, his trials are blessings, his conflicts are victories, his death is immortality, his future is a heaven of inconceivable, unthought-of, untold, and endless blessedness—with such a God, such a Saviour, and such a hope, is he not, ought he not, to be a joyful man?[24]

Someone has come into our lives who is greater and far more joyful than Raymond Chauvet, the stern and vitriolic preacher. Jesus has declared that his joy will be in us and that our joy will be full. With "such a Savior, and such a hope, are we not, ought we not, to be a joyful people? May the joy of heaven fill our hearts and flood our churches, for the glory of Christ alone.

---

[24] From *The Sympathy of Christ with Man*, quoted in Randy Alcorn, *Happiness* (Carol Stream, IL: Tyndale House Publishers, 2015), 23.

4

GRATITUDE
ABOUNDING IN THANKSGIVING

Ben Kreps

Lead Pastor, Living Hope Church (Middletown, PA)

M any of us have gone through the same familiar and very disappointing experience. You start up the car and the dreaded "check-engine" light flickers to life on your dashboard. What could it be? A sensor gone bad? The onset of total engine failure and impending financial ruin? Whatever the cause, we are wise to head to the mechanic and have an expert run a diagnostic test to discern the nature of the problem.

When it comes to the condition of our hearts, we should perceive a warning light that flashes bright red whenever gratitude gives way to grumbling and complaining in our lives. Here's why: gratitude is an essential indicator of how well we apprehend the grace and goodness of God. When gratitude is absent, we must get to the bottom of it.

Maybe it's time for a simple check-up or maybe an opportunity for a major overhaul. Whatever the case, let's allow our hearts to be diagnosed and addressed by the one who knows our hearts better than we do. Let's consider what God's Word says about gratitude and how we can increasingly be shaped to experience and express daily the gratitude and thanksgiving that is his due.

God's Word on Gratitude

It is fitting and appropriate to give thanks to God, for "he himself gives to all mankind life and breath and everything" (Acts 17:25), and "Every good gift and every perfect gift is from above, coming down from the Father of lights" (Jas. 1:17). We are called to recognize that everything we have is a gift from God and therefore our gratitude is to be directed toward God. Furthermore, throughout Scripture we find repeated exhortations such as "Oh give thanks to the Lord; call upon his name; make known his deeds among the peoples" (1 Chr. 16:8)! And, "Oh give thanks to the Lord, for he is good, for his steadfast love endures forever" (Ps. 107:1)!

To be clear, gratitude is not something that only believers experience. Even a hardened atheist can feel grateful in the presence of immense beauty like the Grand Canyon or in the sweet, daily bursts of brilliance as the sun rises and sets. In fact, it is common in our culture to see gratitude as a virtue worth lauding as it brings emotional and physical benefits when cultivated. In the end though, that kind of gratitude is ultimately worthless because a godless gratitude fails to direct our hearts to the one to whom thanksgiving and honor is due.

Tragically, there is a fundamental issue at the heart of fallen men and women—a hardened heart towards God that refuses to express gratitude toward him. The apostle Paul addresses this as he begins his letter to the Romans. In ourselves, we are sinners who stand under the righteous wrath of God and ingratitude is at the core of our rebellion. He writes, "For although they knew God, they did not honor him as God or give thanks to him, but they became futile in their thinking, and their foolish hearts were darkened" (Rom. 1:21). This should correct any impulse to think of ingratitude as merely a character deficiency, a sort of semi-acceptable sin. A failure to honor and thank God describes those who will experience God's judgment. Elsewhere in Scripture ingratitude is listed with arrogance, brutality, and self-centered love as particular hallmarks of those who deny the power of God (2 Tim. 3:1–5). Gratitude is serious business! It is serious because failure to give thanks to God is failure to honor and glorify the one who created us and who daily provides for us. That is negligence of the most arrogant sort.

In light of our many sins, including our failure to appropriately live a lifestyle of thanksgiving toward our generous Creator, it is stunning, amazing grace that God's response to our sin was to send what is most dear to him—his own willing Son. Jesus came to his own and his own did not receive him. He was despised and rejected by those who should have received him with grateful hearts. And yet, he came to save us from our sins, including our ungratefulness. In and through his atoning death as our substitute and through his glorious resurrection, our Savior has defeated sin and death and has opened wide the door to heaven through his body so that formerly ungrateful, ungodly, undeserving sinners like you and me can know the grace, forgiveness, and mercy of God.

In light of this mercy and grace from God, we have endless reasons for profound gratitude in every and any season. In Christ, we may rightly declare, "He has raised my soul from death to life! My sins are washed away! I am an adopted child of God! I have been transferred out the kingdom of darkness into the kingdom of light! My future is glorious!" How can we not be grateful? And so, understandably, the author of Hebrews writes, "Therefore let us be grateful for receiving a kingdom that cannot be shaken, and thus let us offer to God acceptable worship, with reverence and awe" (Heb. 12:28).

In light of the grace of God in Christ, we are exhorted: "Therefore, as you received Christ Jesus the Lord, so walk in him, rooted and built up in him and established in the faith, just as you were taught, *abounding in thanksgiving*" (Col. 2:6–7, emphasis mine). "Abounding in thanksgiving" should describe each and every man, woman, and child who has received and understands the immensity of God's mercy and grace.

Challenges to Gratitude

While gratitude is an appropriate and natural response to the grace of God, our daily experience may fall short of the command given in 1 Thessalonians 5:18: "Give thanks in all circumstances; for this is the will of God in Christ Jesus for you." As we navigate our busy and complicated lives, we may, at times, find an increasing absence of gratitude in the face of real concerns and temptation. In his helpful book *Practicing Thankfulness,* Sam Crabtree writes,

> Just as a fire eventually flickers and dies out if untended, gratitude can easily weaken and fade away if ignored in a

world of distractions, busyness, and painful troubles. Daily life throws cold water on the smoldering embers of gratefulness in our hearts.[25]

When we find it difficult to obey an exhortation like "giving thanks always and for everything to God the Father in the name of our Lord Jesus Christ" (Eph. 5:20), we see once again the dashboard of our hearts light up red. The good news is that we are not stuck! By God's grace we can rekindle and add fuel to the smoldering embers of our gratitude.

Cultivating Gratitude

Author and pastor C.J. Mahaney asks a probing question to help us discern our hearts when he writes:

> What would happen if I crossed your path tomorrow morning? Would I encounter someone who was an alert and thankful observer of answered prayer, someone who in a pronounced way was grateful for God's many mercies? We also want to continue throughout the day expressing gratefulness for the innumerable manifestations of God's grace. It's as if God is placing sticky-notes in our lives everywhere. How alert and perceptive of them are you?[26]

Don't you want to be known as someone who is alert and thankful for the innumerable manifestations of God's mercy and grace that

---

[25] Sam Crabtree, *Practicing Thankfulness* (Wheaton, IL: Crossway Publishing, 2021), 13.
[26] C.J. Mahaney, *Humility* (Sisters, OR: Multnomah Publishers, 2005), 71.

fill our lives each day? If so, let me suggest four ways to cultivate gratitude:

1. Have a conversation with those who know you best.

If we want to cultivate gratitude, we are wise to invite the input of others. Because it is possible to be deceived in our own self-assessment, a humble Christian is wise to invite honest feedback as an opportunity to grow in faithfulness to God. Ask your spouse, your children, or trusted friends, "Do you think I'm a grateful person?" Set aside any defensiveness you may be tempted to feel in the face of criticism and position your mind and heart to listen and consider what those who love you have to say.
I understand that it can be difficult to open ourselves up to potential criticism and correction. But Scripture offers a great promise to those who humble themselves: "God opposes the proud but gives grace to the humble" (Jas. 4:6). When we humble ourselves and are willing to deal honestly and openly with our lives, we should have a happy expectation that we will experience fresh grace from God to sanctify and strengthen our hearts for our growth in gratefulness and godliness.

2. List your benefits.

When the psalmist urges his own soul to bless and praise God in Psalm 103, he begins by listing the benefits that God has given him by his grace.

> Bless the LORD, O my soul, and forget not all his benefits, who forgives all your iniquity, who heals all your diseases, who redeems your life from the pit, who crowns you with

steadfast love and mercy, who satisfies you with good so
that your youth is renewed like the eagle's (Ps. 103:2b–5).

In busyness, distractions, and painful trials we can forget the
goodness and generosity of God. We can forget the immeasurable
grace and benefits that we experience each day. As a result, we
begin to doubt that God is good and faithful. One important way
that we do battle against the temptation to think hard thoughts
about God is to address our souls and regularly rehearse the
bountiful blessings that we have experienced from God. Take some
unhurried time to make a list of benefits that you have received
from God. Psalm 103 is a good starting point, but a thoughtful list
of benefits received will be substantially longer and ever growing
as we remember that "He who did not spare his own Son but gave
him up for us all, how will he not also with him graciously give us
all things" (Rom. 8:32)?

Keep your list at the ready for the inevitable difficult seasons you
will experience throughout your life so that you will be armed
with the truth of God's goodness and faithfulness in order to battle
doubt and fear. When our hearts are aware of God's blessing on
our lives, we will find reasons to sing and praise God even in the
darkness and disillusionment of suffering.

3. Fill your prayers with gratitude.

Consider your prayer life. Are your times in prayer mostly about
expressing desire and need or is there a discernible gratitude that
saturates your prayer? Dependent prayer that shares our needs and
requests to God is vital, but we must not forget that the apostle
Paul instructs every believer, "Continue steadfastly in prayer, being

watchful in it with thanksgiving" (Col. 4:2). In Philippians 4:6 he writes, "Do not be anxious about anything, but in everything by prayer and supplication with thanksgiving let your requests be made known to God."

My grandmother, who passed into the presence of Christ several years ago, knew a lot about suffering and loss and yet she was perhaps the most grateful person I have ever known. She had a rare and sweet ability to see God's goodness in the smallest things each day and she could be heard throughout the day thanking God out loud. Her gracious and grateful heart modeled the call held out for us all to give thanksgiving to God forever and ever (Rev. 7:12). As we approach God in prayer, let us cultivate a gracious heart that is attuned the mercy of God no matter our condition and let us thank God each day for his mercies.

"Whatever You Do..."

Colossians 3:17 exhorts us: "And whatever you do, in word or deed, do everything in the name of the Lord Jesus, giving thanks to God the Father through him." In both words of gratefulness and deeds of love, let us make it our aim to cultivate an awareness of God's grace and activity in our lives and those around us—for the health of our hearts, the encouragement of others, and the glory of the one who has generously and bountifully blessed us in every way. Let us give thanks with grateful hearts as we make our way toward our blessed hope in the day of Christ. For on that day we will join the chorus of heaven in the presence of the Lord singing,

"Blessing and glory and wisdom and thanksgiving and honor and power and might be to our God forever and ever! Amen" (Rev. 7:12). Let's not wait for that great day to start singing; let's join in that song today!

5

ENCOURAGEMENT
CELEBRATING EVIDENCES OF GRACE

Kyle Huber

Lead Pastor, Greentree Church (Egg Harbor Township, NJ)

One of the most unexamined descriptions of God is found in Romans 15:5, where the One we worship and serve is called "the God of endurance and encouragement." God is by nature and practice an encourager! He is openhanded with encouragements to us because we need them in order to endure in joyful faithfulness to him. If God as encourager does not fit how we think about his orientation toward us, we will likely fail to value encouragement as God does. We will consider encouragement as a nice bonus we may hand out to fellow-believers at times, but we will not view encouragement as an integral part of what it means to be Christian.

A Pervasive Theme

The theme of encouragement flows through Scripture because it flows forth from God. When the Lord raised up leaders to serve his people, he called for them to be encouraged (Deut. 3:28, 2 Chr. 35:2). When the church gathers, its members are called to "encourage one another" (1 Thess. 5:11). When Bibles are opened, encouragement is meant to follow (Acts 13:15). Encouragement was one reason why men were sent by the apostles to visit the churches (Eph. 6:22). We are to encourage the "fainthearted" when we encounter them (1 Thess. 5:14). As love grows between us, encouragement should follow (Col. 2:2). And encouragements should commonly be present among those who take Jesus seriously (Phil. 2:1).

So what precisely is this encouragement? There are worldly encouragements that unbelievers give. But true, biblical encouragement is lifting up the saints by holding up Christ and his gospel treasure in order to strengthen them for joyful service to him.

Christ-Centered Encouragement

We all need Christ-centered encouragement because we all experience opposition to Great-Commandment living. We are continually made aware of our ever-present weakness, and we can be overwhelmed by the task of serving Christ in a world filled with challenges. We are tempted to nod in agreement with Thomas Hobbes' infamous statement declaring that life is "nasty, brutish and short."[27] (And you thought it was just you!)

These obstacles to living whole-heartedly for Christ are not impersonal. There is someone actively working against us. His name is Satan, which means the Accuser. He prowls, roars, and devours (1 Pet. 5:8). He sets snares, has schemes, and uses trickery. He is not invincible, but he is persistent. No saint of God is immune to these difficulties. Indeed, each one is tempted to

---

[27] Thomas Hobbes, *Leviathan* (Routledge: Longman Library of Primary Sources in Philosophy, 2016), 9.

weariness and self-doubt. The most fruitful Christian you know very likely feels as though their life is poorly used and ineffectual on a regular basis.

Christ-centered encouragement is not shelling out shallow coffee mug quotations or positive statements that are meant to move the conversation along to safer and more pleasant territory. It is meant to help fellow believers stand against the effects of the fall, to strengthen them to persist in the call to be salt and light. Biblical encouragers are not blind to the world that Hobbes saw around him. Rather, we see that and more. We see Christ and the need to have our hearts filled with confidence in his hold on our lives. We recognize the types of encouragements that will have a meaningful impact on the hearts of those who prize the Savior.

It's Not Beyond Us

When we look at the size of people's burdens, we are tempted to think that any encouragement we have to give is too thin to make much difference. This brings us back to the definition of biblical encouragement, lifting up Christ to those who belong to Christ. Pointing to Christ in meaningful ways is never thin because he is wondrous in every way. There is no glimpse of Christ that is thin in glory or void of meaning. As we point to Christ, we can open the vast treasury of his gospel—the glorious realities which make other forms of inspiration look shabby and tarnished. Reminding people about the sustaining and refreshing truths of Christ doesn't require exaggeration or clever word-smithing. We just give the facts—the jaw-dropping facts—of creation, incarnation, crucifixion, redemption, justification, reconciliation, adoption, sanctification, consolation, glorification, presentation, and celebration.

Encouragement is enjoyable because it identifies the evidences of grace that are already embedded and flowering in the lives of God's people. Encouragement is not a makeshift attempt to stick Christian slogans onto an otherwise pathetic life. Just the opposite! We encourage believers by identifying what is true in them. We brush off the dust and point to the gem. We give voice to the evidential presence of the Holy Spirit. We acknowledge the vibrant colors of Christ's character. We lay out the manifestations of God's Word that we have observed and experienced. In a very real sense, encouragers are treasure hunters who cry out, "There is Christ! I can see him in you!"

God-Given Means of Encouragement

The ministry of Scripture is the primary means by which we are meant to bring encouragement. Romans 15:4 says, "For whatever was written in former days was written for our instruction, that through endurance and the encouragement of the Scriptures we might have hope." God's Word tells us what the God of our salvation has done, promised, and declared. When we bring biblical truths to weary believers, we bring words of life that were specifically given to revive their soul: words which cannot fail or be improved upon.

Biblical encouragement is not relegated to pastors and teachers. All believers are to utilize the truths of Scripture as instruments of encouragement (1 Thess. 4:18). We all have this Word, true food for our soul, which brings joy amidst our deepest trials and provides certainty in a world that trembles. We don't need to be experts in the nuances of the Bible to know its central message: the gospel. We know the main character to whom all Scripture points: Christ! And we know the purpose of Scripture: to draw us into an ever-deepening relationship with him.

A second means God has given each of us for encouraging one another is our gifting by the Holy Spirit. Consider the definition for spiritual gifts found in 1 Corinthians 12:7, "To each is given the manifestation of the Spirit for the common good." And we see the effects of the Spirit's work two chapters later in Paul's repetition of terms for encouraging and building others up (1 Cor. 14:3, 4, 5, 12, 17, 26). The Spirit works through us in ways designed to benefit the other members of our church. All spiritual gifts are Christ-exalting (it is what the Spirit loves to do) and meant for lifting each other's hearts to be Christ-exalting.

As we live dependent upon the Holy Spirit, engaged in meaningful community, the Spirit will draw out of us the means for encouraging one another. As we look for and announce these graces in action, we encourage those who easily miss or minimize those evidences of God at work.

A third means for encouragement is our mutual faith (Rom. 1:12). Becoming citizens of Christ's kingdom makes us strangers and aliens in this world. A significant source of a believer's discouragement comes from the corruption around us and at times in us. But our faith is rooted in the realities of being "more than conquerors through him who loved us" (Rom. 8:37).

We often moan that our faith is weak, not recognizing its actual supernatural nature. Even when our faith falters in a challenging trial or difficult situation, we lean on the truth of God made flesh, the virgin birth, the bodily resurrection, and the return of Jesus as Judge and King. How can we possibly believe what makes the world snicker? It is because we truly do have supernatural faith! We have enough faith to strengthen those who also believe. And when we see or hear of faith in fellow-believers, we are encouraged in the greater exercise of our own faith. As we speak biblically-authorized and faith-filled words to one another, the soul takes a deep breath that revives our whole being.

The Hindrances We Face

So why do we miss all these important and Christ-exalting opportunities to be encouragers to those God has given us to encourage? Here are some common reasons:

1. We accommodate prideful thoughts.

Pride is always a lurking concern. However, when encouragement is focused on God's grace at work in someone, it is more apt to engender humility.

2. We see people's flaws more easily, and may find it hard to see evidences of grace in them.

Remember, the ultimate goal is to exalt Christ. He is worthy of taking the time to look more carefully. Encouragement doesn't have to wait for godly qualities to reach their ripened maturity. In fact, it is a great time to encourage people when areas of growth are still embryonic. The apostle Paul is a great example to us in 1 Corinthians 1. He will soon enough correct this church in matters of significance, yet he doesn't withhold encouragement despite their immaturity.

3. We see ourselves as truth-tellers.
Obviously, truth-telling is a biblical trait. However, pride may be a significant motivation when we see ourselves as sitting in the role of truth-teller to people's sins. 1 Timothy 5:1 urges us to choose encouragement over rebuke. There are times when rebuke is necessary. However, the truth is that every believer has the grace of God in them. And these gospel graces are the greatest truths about them.

4. The mind-to-mouth challenge.
Quite often, I find that I recognize a word, an attitude, or an action that is commendable. And while I take note of it in my mind, I fail to transition what I noticed into words that edify and encourage. So, encourage yourself with the fact that you can strengthen people to serve Christ by sharing what you see of Christ in them.

5. If we didn't encourage people in the past, it feels awkward to suddenly start now.
This is especially true with the people who know us best. Simply be honest and begin your encouragement by saying, "I have not encouraged you much in the past, but it is an area where God is helping me grow." Keep your mind on the prize, which is the wonderful privilege of strengthening people in their faithfulness to God!

6. We don't think about it.

Becoming an encourager is a habit of grace, which means God wants you to grow in it, and the Holy Spirit will enable you to grow in it. Ask God to help you see evidences of grace, and then give you the courage and words to express what you see.

Practical Helps to Grow

Now that you are (hopefully) eager to be used as an encourager to the saints of God, how should you get started and what should you keep in mind?

Encouragement is not scattering flattery or exaggerated statements on people's lives. It is pointing out the truths about Christ and his gospel that apply to Christians, or that you see at work in them. We are not trying to make people feel better as much as helping them see that Christ is present and faithful.

1. Be as specific as possible.

Rather than telling a volunteer, "Great job today," point out something you noticed and thank them for it. The best encouragements are those that point to the beauty of God at work in specific ways.

2. Internalize God's Word.

Know his attributes and his promises. Fill your heart and mind with meditations that are rich in Christ and his gospel. This will heighten your sensitivity to his influences in people.

3. Pay attention to how believers interact with one another.

Any gathering of the church will present abundant opportunities to see God's grace at work in others. And when you hear of praiseworthy activity in the life of someone you know, mark it down and encourage them with what you learned about God's grace in them.

4. Take advantage of the many means we have for sending encouragement.

In today's culture, cards and letters make an impression. Texts are an easy way to connect with people, and may be a helpful way for those who are too shy to bring up encouragements face to face. However, don't neglect in-person encouragements, especially in those moments when you notice behavior that is particularly worthy of it.

5. Review your prayer list and consider who you can reach out to.

Let them know that you carry them on your heart. Include something of the Lord's faithfulness, and don't forget to point out faithfulness you see in how they carry their burdens.

6. Don't wait for big reasons for encouragement.

Just being consistent in living for Christ is worthy of encouragement. Lift up as much as you can, as often as you can.

7. Include encouragements to those you think are mature and don't need it.

The Accuser may be his most furious in attacking them. Every believer is confronted with reasons for discouragement on a regular basis.

8. Be quick to speak up about what God is doing in and around you.

The enemy whispers that God is not all that active in our lives. We need to counter that treacherous voice by helping each other become aware of the fact that God truly is quite active among us!

Encouragement is not just a nice habit; it is part of your biblical faithfulness. And it is a means by which we can be used by God as he cares for and strengthens his people. Take time to think specifically about who you can encourage and why.

A Final Word

There are forms of expertise that are beyond our gifting, but encouragement is not one of them. Each of us can become an expert in identifying evidences of grace in other saints. We all splash about in the ocean of God's grace, and the Holy Spirit is a fountain of grace within us. There are plenty of people fulfilling the role of critic, but the stage is wide open for those who would be encouragers. And when it comes to Christ-exalting encouragers, there can never be too many!

6

GENEROSITY

GOD LOVES CHEERFUL GIVERS

Chad Haygood

Senior Pastor, Grace Life Church (Hastings, NE)

O nly a few years after my conversion, I fell into a trap
common for new converts: the trap of morbid
introspection. The joy of receiving new life in Christ quickly gave
way to despair in my pursuit of holiness. I was burdened by my
lack of growth and despaired the presence of sin that remained in
my life. Despite experiencing the grace of God in Christ only a few
years prior, I was miserable.

The main instrument God used to deliver me from my despair was
a small book many of us are familiar with, *The Cross Centered Life* by
C.J. Mahaney. God used this book as a key to unlock the door in
the room of despair. I realized that, while trusting the gospel for
my salvation, I was not living according to that same gospel.
I discovered that I needed the gospel daily. This small book proved
to be huge in helping me apply the gospel to my growth in Christ.

I soon realized that the Christian life is meant to be marked by
gratitude and joy, not gloom and despair. I understood that
following our Lord was a delight, not a mere duty. I found that,

because of the cross, we can be happy in our sanctification though never satisfied with our present degree of conformity to Christ.

One surprising effect of my new application of the gospel was the joy that I discovered through generosity. Once a greedy, covetous, and selfish man, the gospel taught me that it is truly more blessed to give than to receive (Acts 20:35). In short, I came to realize that gospel people are generous people. We delight in generosity because God has been incomprehensibly generous to us.

Since joining Sovereign Grace in 2015 through the church adoption process, I have been amazed at the abundant generosity that is consistently on display through our churches. In what follows, I hope to outline what I believe are the motives of this expression and how we can continue to pursue a gospel-fueled generosity together.

The Motivation for Generosity

Gospel people are generous people because the gospel displays God's generosity in unfathomable ways. We have been redeemed from our sins and the eternal judgment they deserve because God is generous. He gave generously, joyfully, and sacrificially. He gave his own Son, who in turn gave his own life to rescue us from our sins. This overwhelming generosity is at the heart of one of the Bible's most famous verses: "For God so loved the world, that he gave his only Son, that whoever believes in him should not perish but have eternal life" (John 3:16).

God gave so that we would receive. As we marvel at his generosity toward us, we are transformed into his image, with large and generous hearts. Consider these words from Charles Spurgeon:

> Now, the Lord is the most cheerful of all givers. I want you to think of that for a minute. "Who spared not his own Son." Oh, what a gift was that! Mothers, could you give your sons? Fathers, could you spare your children? Well, yes, perhaps you might for your country, but you could not for your enemies. But God, the cheerful giver, spared not his own Son, but delivered him up for us all, as saith the word. And since then what a cheerful giver he has been! He has given without our asking. We did not ask him to make the covenant of grace. We did not ask him to elect us. We did not ask him to redeem us. These things were done before we were born. We did not ask him to call us by his grace, for, alas! We did not know the value of that call, and we were dead in trespasses and sins, but he gave to us freely of his unsought, but boundless love.[28]

True generosity is not motivated by guilt or even by need. True generosity is motivated by the gospel of grace as it grips our hearts while we behold the incomprehensible generosity of God. His generosity is spoken of again in 2 Corinthians 8:9, "For you know the grace of our Lord Jesus Christ, that though he was rich, yet for your sake became poor, so that you by his poverty might become

---

[28] Charles Spurgeon, "A Cheerful Giver Beloved of God," in *The Metropolitan Tabernacle Pulpit Sermons, vol. 14* (London: Passmore & Alabaster, 1868), 573.

rich." Jesus became poor (Luke 9:58) so that we might become infinitely rich in grace.

Stories and pictures of the broken, abused, neglected, and poor (especially children!) may move tender hearts toward generosity, but nothing transforms a stingy heart more than considering our broken and bleeding Savior, crucified for us. We become generous as we are amazed by our own salvation. The first place we look to motivate our generosity is the gospel of Jesus Christ.

Randy Alcorn said it this way: "Gaze upon Christ long enough, and you'll become more of a giver. Give long enough, and you'll become more like Christ."[29]

The Joy of Generosity

The gospel not only inspires the action of generosity, but also inspires the manner of generosity. By his grace, God replaces begrudging generosity with joy-filled giving. God loves a cheerful giver (2 Cor. 9:7) and he gives us grace so that we can do what he loves! (2 Cor. 8:1)

The apostle Paul gives us an example of joy-filled generosity in 2 Corinthians 8. There, he is challenging the church in Corinth by the example of the church in Macedonia. Paul was eager to support the saints in Jerusalem as they suffered in poverty and was calling upon fellow Christians elsewhere to contribute to their financial need. Paul wanted the church in Jerusalem's needs to be met through the giving of the Corinthians and others.

---

[29] Randy Alcorn, *The Treasure Principle* (Sisters, OR: Multnomah, 2001), 30.

In an effort to solicit their support, Paul tells the Corinthians about the support that was given from the church in Macedonia. He says, in 2 Corinthians 8:1–4,

> We want you to know, brothers, about the grace of God that has been given among the churches of Macedonia, for in a severe test of affliction, their abundance of joy and their extreme poverty have overflowed in a wealth of generosity on their part. For they gave according to their means, as I can testify, and beyond their means, of their own accord, begging us earnestly for the favor of taking part in the relief of the saints.

The Macedonians, while facing severe tests of affliction and extreme poverty, gave generously. Notice the manner of their giving as well, they had an abundance of joy as they gave. They were so cheerful in their giving that they begged the apostle to let them give. We might have looked at this church and said, "No, don't you worry about giving. You have needs of your own." But they insisted on giving and were joyful about it.

God cares deeply about our motivations in generosity. He does not want us to give out of compulsion, guilt, or pride. He wants us to delight in giving. God delights in hearts that delight to give. Hearts that have been transformed by the gospel are transformed all the way down to the affections that prompt joyful, selfless generosity.

The Reward of Generosity

God is so delighted when his people give cheerfully that he rewards their joy by enabling them to give even more! Imagine an investment that always yields a fruitful return; this is what joyful generosity is like. God rewards our generosity with a supply that enables us to give more.

> Honor the Lord with your wealth and with the firstfruits of all your produce; then your barns will be filled with plenty and your vats will be bursting with wine (Prov. 3:9–10).

> Whoever is generous to the poor lends to the Lord, and he will repay him for his deed (Prov. 19:17).

As I write this article, the farmers in Nebraska are preparing for planting season. Equipment is being prepared, fertilizer is being sprayed, and rain is being prayed for. In mid-April, our farmers will be laboring in their fields to plant seed that will be harvested, Lord willing, in October. This is a critical time for our farmers because their livelihoods depend on the coming harvest this fall.

Paul uses this farming illustration to teach the Corinthians about generosity in 2 Corinthians 9. He says, "The point is this: whoever sows sparingly will also reap sparingly, and whoever sows bountifully will also reap bountifully" (2 Cor. 9:6). This is a simple equation for agriculture: if you sow a little seed this April you will reap a little harvest this fall. If you sow bountifully, you will also reap bountifully.

When we consider our own generosity, we are tempted to approach it like an accountant. We wonder how much it will cost us to give and measure our giving in light of our personal needs or the needs of our family. John Calvin warns us about this in his commentary on 2 Corinthians 8.

> For what makes us more close-handed than we ought to
> be is—when we look too carefully, and too far forward, in
> contemplating the dangers that may occur—when we are
> excessively cautious and careful—when we calculate too
> narrowly what we will require during our whole life, or,
> in fine, how much we lose when the smallest portion is
> taken away. The man, that depends upon the blessing of
> the Lord, has his mind set free from these trammels, and
> has, at the same time, his hands opened for beneficence.[30]

When we focus our concerns on our temporary or future needs to determine our generosity, we fail to realize that God will supply all our needs. He has a higher goal in mind than just meeting our needs. He will provide so that we will have all that we need and opportunity to continue our generous giving.

> And God is able to make all grace abound to you, so that
> having all sufficiency in all things at all times, you may
> abound in every good work. As it is written, 'He has
> distributed freely, he has given to the poor; his
> righteousness endures forever.' He who supplies seed to
> the sower and bread for food will supply and multiply your
> seed for sowing and increase the harvest of your
> righteousness. You will be enriched in every way to be

---

[30] John Calvin and John Pringle, *Commentaries on the Epistles of Paul the Apostle to the Corinthians, vol. 2* (Bellingham: Logos Bible Software, 2010), 285–286.

generous in every way, which through us will produce thanksgiving to God. (2 Cor. 9:8–11)

Theologian Charles Hodge said,

> The main idea the apostle designs to present as having the sanction of the word of God is, that he who is liberal, who disperses, scatters abroad his gifts with free-handed generosity, as a man scatters seed, shall always have abundance.[31]

Our reward extends beyond our return as well. The additional, and primary reward is the praise of God that our generosity elicits.

> You will be enriched in every way to be generous in every way, which through us will produce thanksgiving to God. For the ministry of this service is not only supplying the needs of the saints but is also overflowing in many thanksgivings to God. By their approval of this service, they will glorify God because of your submission that comes from your confession of the gospel of Christ, and the generosity of your contribution for them and for all others, while they long for you and pray for you, because of the surpassing grace of God upon you. (2 Cor. 9:11–14)

The result of our generosity is not just that needs will be met, missionary endeavors are funded, or buildings are built. Giving

---

[31] Charles Hodge, *A Commentary on 1 and 2 Corinthians* (Carlisle, PA: The Banner of Truth Trust, 1974), 597.

generously promotes gratitude towards God and brings glory to him!

Living Generously

With gratitude in our hearts and promises in our hands, we can travel the road of joyful and abundant generosity. Because of what Christ has done and the promises he offers to us, the entirety of our lives should be marked by generosity. A generous heart not only impacts our bank accounts, but our time and talents as well.

When I accepted the call to be a pastor in Nebraska, my young family moved from our home and extended families in Alabama, one thousand miles away. Since we arrived, a dear lady from our church insisted on watching our children (now 4 of them) regularly (for free!) so that Meredith and I can enjoy a date night. Another family invites us to their home every Easter so that we will not spend that day alone. These families are rich in good works (2 Tim. 6:18). They are generous with their time and talents.

Hospitality, counsel, sharing, and many other expressions of love require generosity. God rewards and is praised by all of them. We should be eager to do good to everyone, and especially those in the household of faith (Gal. 6:10). Do not grow weary in it; God will reward you in due time (Gal. 6:9).

Let me encourage you with several ways that you can experience the joy of generosity.

1. Fix your heart on Christ. Remember that he was born, broken, buried, and raised for you. By his wounds you have been healed. You are born again because God is generous (Eph. 2:4–5).

2. Be rich in good works. Serve others. Find ways to serve your church. Be hospitable. Do good to those in need (Prov. 3:27–28).

3. Give when it seems unreasonable. Be sacrificial. Do not let your circumstances hinder your generosity. Give when it seems impossible (2 Cor. 8:2–3).

4. Support your church's mission. Give so that churches can be planted through Sovereign Grace (Rom. 15:24).

Conclusion

I am so thankful to call Sovereign Grace Churches my home. I am indebted to the gospel centrality that I have learned from men in Sovereign Grace. I have been the beneficiary of enormous generosity in our partnership. May the legacy laid before us continue, with hearts full of gratitude to God and hands open with generosity toward others.

7

SERVANTHOOD

"LET ME BE AS CHRIST TO YOU"

Greg Dirnberger

Senior Pastor, Emmaus Road Church (Sioux Falls, SD)

A s someone who came alive to Christ during the "Jesus Movement" in the 70's, certain songs contributed to my spiritual developmental. One such song was Richard Gillard's simple chorus, "The Servant Song." I chuckle now to think back on how mellow and tender-hearted our college fellowship was when we sang together, "Will you let me be your servant, let me be as Christ to you? Pray that I may have the grace to let you be my servant too."[32]

I'm also astonished and a bit ashamed to say that the servant-oriented impulse of my early years as a Christ-follower diminished as I engaged in vocational pastoral ministry. I certainly understood servanthood to be a disposition of all true Christ-followers. I had taught that to "serve one another" was an expression of loving your neighbor as yourself. Certainly "service" was a spiritual gift. And in my tradition, we often said to one another, "If there's anything you need me to do, just ask."

---

[32] Richard Gillard. "The Servant Song" Scripture in Song, 1977.

However, until I encountered the virtue of servanthood, manifest so consistently in my interactions with Sovereign Grace people, I would have perceived "service" as a lesser gift. I would have considered it more likely an expression of mature emotional intelligence. I would have thought of it, mainly, as a winsome trait which organizations (including churches) gained through effective customer service training, but not necessarily as a fruit of the functional centrality of the gospel. My perspective has changed.

"How can I serve you?" "Would it serve you if I . . ." "We're here to serve." "It is pure joy for us to serve you." I expect that members and regular attenders of Sovereign Grace churches immediately recognize this vernacular. But until I engaged with Sovereign Grace folk for the first time in 2006, those words were not in my parlance.

We naturally tend to emulate those we admire. I suspect that servanthood, both its vocabulary and practice, have become more discernible in my life, on account of the high regard I have for those who have served my wife and me so well since we joined Sovereign Grace Churches eleven years ago. Servanthood is something we have "caught."

However, it's also clear that servanthood is not merely something we "catch." Servanthood is a distinct virtue born of gospel doctrine, and produced in our lives through the active work of God the Holy Spirit.

Servanthood Displayed and Commended

In the final section of his majestic letter to "all those in Rome who are loved by God and called to be saints" (Rom. 1:7), the apostle Paul commends several individuals for their outstanding acts of service. There is "Phoebe, a servant of the church at Cenchreae" (Rom. 16:1), someone whom he exhorts the Roman Christians to help "in whatever way she may need" (Rom. 16:2). Paul sends greetings to Prisca and Aquilla, his "fellow workers in Christ Jesus" (Rom. 16:3), whom he says, "risked their necks" for his life (Rom. 16:4). Then there are Tryphaena and Tryphosa whom Paul identifies as "workers in the Lord," as well as Persis "who has worked hard in the Lord" (Rom. 16:12). Paul draws attention to the mother of Rufus, who had been like a mother to Paul as well (Rom. 16:13).

From the "calling up" of those listed in this brief roster, we learn that servanthood includes helping people in need, risk-taking for others' good, hard work on others' behalf, and mother-like care. Paul attributes the same virtue to Titus, a fellow worker for others' benefit (2 Cor. 8:23), and Philemon whom he commends for refreshing the hearts of the saints (Phlm. 7).

Servanthood, then, seems to be a somewhat broad category for actively and intentionally pursuing the benefit and well-being of others. And though the apostle Paul attributes servanthood to a vast array of people, who serve in a variety of ways" (1 Cor. 12:5), the consummate display of servanthood is witnessed in the person and life of the Lord Jesus Christ.

During his final meal with his twelve disciples, Jesus famously knelt down and donned a towel to communicate that the purpose of his coming was not to be served, but rather to serve and to lay down his life, sacrificially, as ransom for many. His entire aim was our ultimate well-being. That is, to cleanse us from the filth and shame of our sin, and to restore us to a right relationship with the Father. And further, his purpose was that we might watch and learn from his sacrifice, and to love and serve one another in a similar way. Jesus said,

> You call me Teacher and Lord, and you are right, for so I am. If I then, your Lord and Teacher, have washed your feet, you also ought to wash one another's feet. For I have given an example, that you also should do just as I have done to you (John 13:13–15, see also Mark 10:43–45).

It would seem clear that it is impossible to yield to Christ's lordship and follow him whole-heartedly without servanthood being evident in our lives. The less we're inclined to serve, the less like Jesus we are.

Servanthood Commanded

To serve, then, is a gospel claim on the life of every believer. Paul writes, "Through love serve one another. For the whole law is fulfilled in one word: "You shall love your neighbor as yourself" (Gal. 5:13b–14). It is right to understand servanthood as a powerful and practical means of building up a spiritual community. He writes again,

There are varieties of service, but the same Lord, and
there are varieties of activities, but it is the same God who
empowers them all in everyone. To each is given the
manifestation of the Spirit for the common good
(1 Cor. 12:5–7).

To the Romans, Paul says, "Having gifts that differ according to the
grace given to us, let us use them . . . if service, in our serving"
(Rom. 12:6–7).

Nevertheless, servanthood is also more than a useful "gift" given to
and exercised by some. Servanthood is an evidence of God's saving
grace. The apostle John writes,

We know that we have passed out of death into life,
because we love the brothers . . . By this we know love,
that he laid down his life for us, and we ought to lay down
our lives for the brothers (1 John 3:14, 16).

Servanthood is a gospel issue. In Luke 10:25–37, a lawyer comes to
Jesus and asks him the most important question in the world.
"What must I do to inherit eternal life?" Jesus answers the man
with a question. "What does the Bible say? How do you interpret
it?" The lawyer, being the knowledgeable person he was, says that
the biblical basis for salvation can be summed up in the commands,
"You shall love the Lord your God with all your heart and with all
your soul and with all your mind, and your strength and with all
your mind, and your neighbor as yourself" (Luke 10:27).

But Jesus, the discerner of hearts, knows that the lawyer's agenda springs from a desire to justify himself. What he really wants to know is, "Who don't I have to love?" "What is the bare minimum I have to do to inherit eternal life?" But the question Jesus wants the lawyer, and us, to ask is, "Who can I be a neighbor to today?" Who can I serve? To whom can I be as Christ?

This is profoundly instructive in shaping the gospel virtue of servanthood. The only ones who will inherit eternal life are those who are learning to love their neighbors as themselves.

According to the Great Commandment, there are two kinds of love. One is the way we love God. That is, loving with all our whole being. Since God has no needs and is utterly self-sufficient (Acts 17:24–25; Ps. 50:9–11), we don't love him by giving him anything, meeting his needs, or satisfying his longings. We love God by delighting in him. We love him by enjoying him with heart, soul, strength and mind, as the object of our pleasure.

The other way to love is by meeting needs, showing kindness, bearing burdens, and being merciful. In other words, we love by serving. That is, we love the way we love ourselves. Scripture assumes what we already know this. There's no one on earth who hates his own flesh. By nature, we are utterly devoted to nourishing, and cherishing, and earnestly pursuing our own well-being (Eph. 5:29). Do you want to know what servanthood looks like? Consider how concerned and committed we are to meeting our own needs, then do that for others.

Servanthood and the Functional Centrality
of the Gospel

Self-centered love of ourselves is perhaps the most significant obstacle to servanthood. When my first impulse is to actively pursue my own well-being, I'm faced with two problems. One, I quickly recognize my limitations in accomplishing that goal. I'm a "black hole" of need. Satisfying all my self-serving desires is impossible when relying upon me alone. If I'm insufficient to meet my own needs, how (and why) would I offer myself and my resources to meet the needs of others? Second, I'm far less motivated to involve myself in serving, and caring, and meeting the needs of others if I'm anxious about my own needs being met. I want. I have limitations. Perhaps I won't get what I want.

This is where it becomes more obvious that the best way to love ourselves is to love God with all our being: value him, entrust ourselves to him, and pursue our soul-satisfaction in him. When I believe that all that I need for my peace and joy will be supplied by my faithful, all-sufficient, infinitely competent, steadfastly loving heavenly Father, then I'm set free from insisting that I get what I want exactly when I want it. I'm content in trusting that he is pursuing my best interests with goodness and mercy all the days of my life. And I'm confident that he will do so, because he has purchased the guarantee of the fulfillment of every promise he has made to me, in the death of his dearly loved Son (2 Cor. 1:20).

Obeying the great and first commandment (Matt. 22:38) is then the best and only way we can love and serve and bless and be actively involved in seeking the joy and well-being of others. In fact, the very best way we love and serve our neighbors (and enemies) is to lead them, by our witness, in word and caring servanthood, to love God with all their being.

Servanthood and Our Family of Churches

My first ever visit to a Sovereign Grace Church happened during WorshipGod 2006. I was staying with a friend who worked in Washington D.C., and who had an apartment in Pentagon City. It was a long Metro ride back and forth. Following the first night of the conference, I stood alone at the bus stop across the street from the church. It was late and dark. As the last car left the church parking lot, they waved me over and asked where I needed to go. When I said the Gaithersburg Metro Station, they offered me a ride.

The next day, I crossed paths with this Sovereign Grace Church family again. They immediately expressed how thankful they were to God that they had found me in the crowd, because they wanted to invite me to be a part of their family for the rest of the week. They took me to their home. They served me dinner each evening of the conference thereafter. They were at the Metro station to meet me in the morning, and they dropped me off again at night. Their generosity, their hospitality, their care, their sacrifice, and perhaps most of all, their discernible joy in meeting my needs left an impression on me that I will never forget.

Of course, we can make servanthood something that we shouldn't. We can turn servanthood into an idol. We can make it a means to feeling good about ourselves. However, serving is part of God's creative design for each of us who have been joined to Christ

(Eph. 2:10). Serving, according to the strength that God supplies glorifies God as the giver (1 Pet. 4:11) and is nourishing to our souls (John 4:34).

If humility is the foundation of the Shaping Virtues of Sovereign Grace Churches, then servanthood is the capstone. It certainly attracted me. It provoked me. It stirred me. It compelled me.

"Let Me Be as Christ to You"

In 2011, the Lord kindly supplied the faith my wife and I needed to leave our jobs and attend the Sovereign Grace Pastors College. In 2013, by God's grace, we planted Emmaus Road Church in Sioux Falls, SD. It has been one of our greatest joys to serve the people whom God has been building together. It has been one of our greatest joys to serve alongside our dearest friends on earth in Sovereign Grace. We have learned that servanthood is the substance of a gospel-centered life.

"[Christ] died for all, that those who live might no longer live for themselves but for him, who for their sake died and was raised" (2 Cor. 5:15).

And now, as that old chorus testifies, "We are pilgrims on the journey. We're together on this road." And as we have seen and learned from God's Word, and from our brothers and sisters in Sovereign Grace, "we are here to help each other walk the mile and bear the load."[33]

---

[33] Richard Gillard. "The Servant Song" Scripture in Song, 1977.

8

GODLINESS
BECOMING MORE LIKE JESUS

Josh Pannell

Pastor, Trinity Fellowship Addis Ababa (Ethiopia)

T hat sinking feeling still lingers in my mind. It seemed that, in
a single moment, I realized that I had everything backward in
my marriage, parenting, and fellowship with other believers. I was
chasing something that wasn't worth an ounce of my energy. I was
chasing the appearance of godliness, but on the inside was nothing
more than weariness: weariness from running after the idol of the
approval from others and approval from myself. The moment I'm
describing was when Jeff Purswell welcomed us to the Sovereign
Grace Pastors College and called our class to put equal emphasis on
growth in theology and godliness that year. I still can't read
1 Timothy 4:16 without hearing Jeff's voice urging me away from
"superficial goodness" and toward a truly transformed life.

Thomas à Kempis summarizes this well when he says,

> What good does it do to speak learnedly about the Trinity
> if, lacking humility, you displease the Trinity? Indeed it is
> not learning that makes a man holy and just, but a
> virtuous life makes him pleasing to God. I would rather

feel contrition than know how to define it. For what would it profit us to know the whole Bible by heart and the principles of all the philosophers if we live without grace and the love of God?[34]

Jeff helped me see that godliness is not the same as doing good things. No, the call to godliness is something far more. Why? Because our sin sinks far below our actions and into the very core of our being—so much so that it's possible to have "the appearance of godliness" (2 Tim. 3:5) but on the inside be "full of greed and self-indulgence," "all uncleanness," and "hypocrisy and lawlessness" (Matt. 23:25, 27–28). Put simply, godliness isn't external conformity; it's wholistic transformation. Jesus wants nothing less than our whole persons to be changed into his likeness — our actions, yes, but more than just our actions. He wants our desires, affections, motives, and imaginations to be wholly and entirely his.

During my time at the Pastors College, God confronted me in my hypocrisy, self-righteousness, and self-deceit. Godliness isn't something I perform; it's a gospel-virtue that the Holy Spirit must work in my heart to make me truly and holistically more like Christ. Godliness isn't just doing the actions of Christ but feeling the very heart of Christ himself as we do them. This is the kind of godliness that only the power of the gospel can produce.

Godliness and Gospel-Security

Foundational to our growth in godliness is knowing and feeling our status as justified sinners. The identity of every Christian is

---

[34] Thomas à Kempis, *The Imitation of Christ* (Oak Harbor, WA: Logos Research Systems, 1996), 1-2.

found not in our obedience but in the glorious truth that, though we are sinners by nature and by action, God declares us to be "not guilty" because of the life, death, and resurrection of Jesus Christ. Theologians refer to this as "justification." Paul notes in Romans 3 that justification is "a gift" (Rom. 3:24) and is received "by faith apart from works of the law" (Rom. 3:28). We who had forfeited a right standing before God with every sinful action, thought, and intent are scandalously declared to be in the right by a holy God. How can this be? The answer is found in Romans 3:24–25, we are justified "through the redemption that is in Christ Jesus, whom God put forward as a propitiation by his blood." When Jesus died on the cross for sinners, he took upon himself the judgment we deserve—the full force of divine wrath against our sin—so that, for every person in Christ, "there is now no condemnation" (Rom. 8:1).

This is why it is after—and only after—we have received acceptance through the gospel that we are then called to live lives "worthy of the gospel" (Phil. 1:27) and to "cleanse ourselves from every defilement of body and spirit" (2 Cor. 7:1). These texts describe not our justification but "sanctification"—the process in which our actions and desires are increasingly brought into conformity with our justified status before God. We become practically who we already are positionally. Why is it essential that we get the order right? Because the fundamental identity of the Christian is never his performance but Christ's. In theological terms, our security before God is never found in our sanctification but only in our justification. We don't obey so that God will love us; we obey because he already loves us.

Justification and sanctification go hand-in-hand in the Christian life, and you can't have one without the other. Why is that? Because this "righteousness of God" that becomes ours in our justification is none other than Christ himself. Jesus himself becomes to us "righteousness" (1 Cor. 1:30), and we who have been joined to Christ receive all of his righteousness because we receive Christ himself. And when we receive Christ, we receive all of him, so that Paul finishes 1 Corinthians 1:30 by saying that Christ has become to us, not just righteousness, but also "sanctification." Receiving Christ means that we not only receive his righteousness but that we also receive his sanctifying power in our lives. Martin Luther describes it like this, "Christ daily drives out the old Adam more and more in accordance with the extent to which faith and knowledge of Christ grow."[35] Sanctification cannot be divorced from justification any sooner than Christ himself can be divided.

Gospel-Empowered Godliness

Because Jesus himself is our sanctification, it is Jesus, and his gospel, that motivates and empowers growth in godliness and wholistic transformation. It is the blood of Jesus that purifies "our conscience from dead works to serve the living God." And it is "the blood of the eternal covenant" (Heb. 9:14) that "equips us with everything good that we may do his will" (Heb. 13:20–21).

---

[35] Else Marie Wiberg Pedersen, "Sermon on Two Kinds of Righteousness," in *Word and Faith*, ed. Hans J. Hillerbrand, Kirsi I. Stjerna, and Timothy J. Wengert, vol. 2, *The Annotated Luther* (Minneapolis, MN: Fortress Press, 2015), 15.

Paul says as much at the end of Titus 2, "The grace of God has appeared...training us to renounce ungodliness and worldly passions, and to live self-controlled, upright, and godly lives" (Titus 2:11–12). When Paul says that grace appeared, he doesn't mean "grace" in the abstract, but grace in a Person: Jesus is grace incarnate. When Jesus came, he brought the grace of God to us in his person, and that grace not only justifies us before God but also "trains us" to live lives of holiness.

Paul says the same thing in Ephesians 5 with the husband-wife analogy. While we may be familiar with the glorious truth that "Christ loved the church and gave himself up for her," the good news is that Jesus' love for his church doesn't end when he saves her through his gospel; no, Christ died for the church "that he might sanctify her" (Eph. 5:25–26). What this means is that Christ's work in us doesn't end when we hear the declaration "no judgment because of Christ," but when we hear, "no spots or blemishes because of Christ." His deep love for his bride didn't end when he died for her. His love is stronger than that. His love is strong enough to bring to completion in us everything that he started in us.

This is the very point Paul makes when he commands the Philippians to obey the commands of God because "it is God who works in you, both to will and to work for his good pleasure" (Phil. 2:12–13). In all the progress we make towards Christlikeness, we say with Paul, "it was not I, but the grace of God that is with me" (1 Cor. 15:10).

The Urgency of Godliness

Against this backdrop of our warrior King conforming us to his own image, the commands of Scripture demand we fight to achieve Christlikeness. Because we know that Christ is defeating all his enemies in our soul, we can confidently face the commands of Scripture which urge us to "walk in a manner worthy of the calling to which you have been called" (Eph. 4:1). The command of God to Israel rings just as true for New Covenant believers,

> Consecrate yourselves, and be holy, for I am holy. You shall not defile yourselves. . .For I am the Lord who brought you up out of the land of Egypt to be your God. You shall therefore be holy, for I am holy (Lev. 11:44–45).

While we are eternally secure in our justified state, it is equally true that "if [we] live according to the flesh [we] will die" (Rom. 8:13) and "that everyone who is sexually immoral or impure, or who is covetous (that is, an idolater), has no inheritance in the kingdom of Christ and God" (Eph. 5:5). The stakes are high, and we're meant to feel them.

This is why, when Paul describes our fight against sin, he says to the Colossian church, "Put to death therefore what is earthly in you" (Col. 3:5). This kind of language calls for radical devotion toward godliness. Killing is a violent act. Killing takes courage; it's not for the faint of heart. After Gideon defeated Midian in Judges 7, he calls Jether, his firstborn son, to personally kill Zebah and Zalmunna, the enemy kings – "Rise and kill them!" (Judg. 8:20). But Jether could not kill them, "for he was afraid." He looked the enemy in the eye and couldn't muster the courage to swing his sword and kill the enemy.[36]

So, too, Christ calls us to something that takes great courage: we must kill sin, the great enemy of our souls. And when the day of mortifying sin comes, we must not be found wanting courage. For if we do, the enemy will continue to wage war against our souls. In the battle against sin, there is room for neither neutrality nor indifference; rather, as John Owen says in *The Mortification of Sin,*

> Indwelling sin is compared to a person, a living person, called "the old man," with his faculties, and properties, his wisdom, craft, subtlety, strength; this, says the apostle, must be killed, put to death, mortified, that is, have its power, life, vigour, and strength, to produce its effects, taken away by the Spirit. . .Do you mortify; do you make it your daily work; be always at it whilst you live; cease not a day from this work; be killing sin or it will be killing you.[37]

Paul himself echoes the urgency of putting sin to death when he says,

> Do not be deceived: God is not mocked, for whatever one sows, that will he also reap. For the one who sows to his own flesh will from the flesh reap corruption, but the one

---

[36] Yeabtsega Haile Tedla, a Trinity Fellowship Pastors College student, drew my attention to this example.

[37] John Owen, *The Works of John Owen*, ed. William H. Goold, vol. 6 (Edinburgh: T&T Clark, n.d.), 8–9.

who sows to the Spirit will from the Spirit reap eternal life (Gal. 6:7–8).

This call to put sin to death in our hearts extends far beyond our actions into our heart desires. Jesus makes this clear when he says, "you therefore must be perfect, as your heavenly Father is perfect" (Matt. 5:48). The word Jesus uses for "perfect" is "τέλειος," meaning "whole" or "complete." Jesus calls his followers to have a righteousness like God's: righteous actions which flow from a righteous heart. This is a radical call for godliness that seeks to eradicate not just the unrighteousness others can see but even the motives and secrets of the heart that wage war against God.

The Means of Godliness

How then do we cultivate this holistic godliness in our hearts? If we are commanded to kill sin, what weapon do we bring into battle to put it to death? This is where Sovereign Grace's shared value of gospel-centrality beautifully meets our shaping virtue of godliness. We put sin to death by intentionally exposing ourselves to the gospel for the purpose of being transformed by the gospel. Paul says as much in Romans 1:16, "the gospel is the power of God to salvation," that is, salvation in all its parts. The gospel has the power to free us, not just from the penalty of sin in our justification but also from the power of sin in our sanctification. The same gospel that pardons us of our sin also accomplishes our sanctification and makes possible godly living.

While there are many avenues of doing this, let me suggest three.

Meditation

First, we expose ourselves to the gospel by meditating on the gospel. When the author to the Hebrews exhorts his audience to "lay aside every weight and the sin which clings so closely," he immediately gives us the means: "looking to Jesus" (Heb. 12:1–2). The picture here is that, as we look to Jesus and his work on the cross in our place, we find that the weights of sin fall off so that we're able to "run with endurance." Immediately following these verses, the author again calls us to "consider him...so that you may not grow weary or fainthearted" (Heb. 12:3). That is to say, we throw off our sins and imitate our Savior as we meditate on the gospel.

Thus, we store the Word in our hearts so it stands at the ready to be applied. The Word illuminates our way forward when tempted. The Word adjusts our fleshly impulses. The Word comforts and assures. We meditate so that we are armed for the battle we face as we cast aside that sin which clings so closely.

Confession

Second, we expose ourselves to the gospel as we confess our sins. The purpose of confession is never self-condemnation but worshipful celebration and fresh reminders that Jesus died for all of our sins on the cross. John reminds us that as we confess our sins, God is faithful, not only "to forgive our sins" but also to "cleanse us from all unrighteousness" (1 John 1:9). What John has in mind is not just forgiveness by means of gospel-centered confession but the eradication of sin and growth in godliness by means of gospel-centered confession.

Thus, we agree with God in our confession those thoughts and actions that are not in keeping with his will. This pattern of confession keeps us close to the cross, keeps us from drifting, and keeps us walking in step with the Spirit. Confession is an essential means toward godliness because through confession we bring our sin into the light.

Community

Third, we expose ourselves to the gospel in community. The church community is given to "stir up one another to love and good works" (Heb. 10:24). But how does the church do this? The answer is by "encouraging one another" to "hold fast to the confession of our hope" (Heb. 10:25), that is, by reminding one another of the gospel and by calling one another to hold fast to the gospel. Paul says the same in Ephesians 4:15 when he calls the church to "[speak] the truth in love" so that we "grow up in every way into...Christ." What truth does Paul have in mind? "The word of truth, the gospel of your salvation" (Eph. 1:13). We grow in godliness as we are faithfully reminded of the gospel by a local community of gospel-centered believers.

Thus, we commit to building our lives with others and allowing them to see us, at our finest and at our worst. We receive correction as wounds from friends. We express suspicion about our own hearts and charity toward others. We accept the discomfort and inconveniences of fellowship in exchange for the great promises of all God declares will come to us and through us in community.

Conclusion

A proper understanding and application of godliness leaves us with a very big view of God and a sober view of sin. The Christ-follower in pursuit of godliness never toys with sin, tolerates its presence, nor cherishes the short-term payoff it promises. Rather, with divine energy and personal relentlessness, the believer habitually meditates upon God's Word, confesses sin, and builds in meaningful community with others. Godliness becomes reality when the gospel is central, not just in our beliefs but also in all our practices. In this way, every ounce of godliness is because of the incredible work of Christ in our lives.

9

HOW PASTORS CAN CULTIVATE OUR SHAPING VIRTUES IN THE LOCAL CHURCH

Rich Richardson

Lead Elder, Center Church (Gilbert, AZ)

A s a new dad, I was shocked and dismayed when my baby boy growled in response to a greeting from a sweet lady in the grocery store. She strode up and fawned over my son's fiery red hair and exclaimed, "How are you, sweetie?"

He came out with a guttural sound from deep within, "GRRRRRRR."

She fixed her shocked dinner-plate-sized eyes and said, "Is he growling at me?"

All I could do was say, "Yes, yes, he is. Sorry."

"Where did he learn that?" was the pressing question that throbbed in my head. Why is my precious boy growling at innocent, sweet old ladies in the cereal aisle? A few days later, I was "wrestling" with him. (He was about six months old and it was mostly me turning him over and over and making him laugh.) While we "wrestled," I heard myself growling. My son had learned to growl from me. What?! Not only did I have no idea that I growled when we wrestled, but my infant son had copied me and was now growling at others. My hyper-attentive son was following my example.

The churches we serve are hyper-attentive to the example their pastors set. As we think about cultivating our Shaping Virtues, we pastors must lead by example. Teaching about these virtues is good. But we must realize that they are more often "caught than taught." Dr. D.A. Carson states,

> If I have learned anything in 35 or 40 years of teaching, it is that students don't learn everything I teach them. What they learn is what I am excited about, the kinds of things I emphasize again and again and again and again.[38]

Our people are watching.

Paul knew this as well and directed the church at Corinth, "Be imitators of me, as I am of Christ" (1 Cor. 11:1). Can you say this? If our people imitate our example, what will they resemble? Genuine

---

[38] Justin Taylor. "Carson: People Don't Learn What I Teach Them; They Learn What I'm Excited About." The Gospel Coalition. https://www.thegospelcoalition.org/blog/justin-taylor

gospel virtues are infectious. If you are excited and emphasize these virtues, your church will embody these virtues. You can emphasize these virtues to your watching church in two primary ways: personally and publicly.

Our Personal Example

When the gospel of Jesus Christ masters us, a torrent of gospel virtues will gush forth from our lives. It would be too mechanical and hypocritical if we just put on a show of modeling these virtues. Pastors are called not merely to act these virtues out, but to take the lead in applying them to ourselves. In Sovereign Grace, we must continue to be a company of pastors who tend to our souls because we know our souls do not tend to themselves. The Scottish pastor, Robert Murray M'Cheyne, said, "My people's greatest need is my personal holiness."[39] He understood that our people will resemble their leaders.

When we apply these virtues to our own lives, the lives of our people will change. When you respond to an angry email with humility, you set an example. When you express joy in the Lord on a dreary Tuesday afternoon, you set an example. When you pour forth gratefulness upon the sound technician, you set an example. When you are more precise with your encouragement than your correction, you set an example. When you generously give your time to a seasoned saint who is shut-in, you set an example. When you call someone who got a cancer diagnosis to pray for them, you set an example. When you mow the lawn of a single mom, you set an example. Paul expressed the same sentiment when he said,

---

[39] Robert Murray M'Cheyne: quoted in Tony Sargent, *The Sacred Anointing* (Wheaton, IL: Crossway Books, 1994), 80.

"Keep a close watch on yourself and the teaching. Persist in this, for by so doing you will save both yourself and your hearers" (1 Tim. 4:16). Humanly speaking, the people we serve depend on the example we set. They will become what we model. What are you modeling personally?

Our Public Example

Every Sunday, when we gather to join our voices with the throng of heaven, pray in the name of the risen Jesus, and preach Christ by the power of the Spirit, we are providing an example. Any pastor who has public responsibility on Sunday has a weekly opportunity to exemplify these virtues. Our people studiously observe what we celebrate and encourage, who we honor and recognize, and how we do both. We can teach the church to be generous, but we make a more significant impact if we show them generosity.

A couple of years ago, we erected a new church sign on our property. Not two weeks later, I was summoned outside on a sweltering Saturday afternoon because a young man was throwing large rocks at the sign. Our sparkling new sign had more craters than the moon by the time I arrived. As I started talking to the young man, it was clear that some sort of mental illness dogged him. He told me that he was angry at God because he could not get any relief. Consequently, he took out his frustrations on our church sign because it reminded him of his disappointment in God. Our pastoral team decided not to press charges but instead paid for him to get professional help for his condition. The man received treatment and started to improve.

When I shared this story with our church, many people said they were so grateful to be a part of such a generous church. Did our team do anything unique? Unprecedented? No, we all know what it is like to be the recipient of the generosity of our Father. All we did was share it with someone else. That story had a more significant impact than any teaching on generosity we have given. Our people are studying our public examples. Even something as pedestrian as announcements is an invitation to impart one of these Shaping Virtues. We cannot afford just to pass along information. Still, announcements can be a means of transformation if we model these virtues. It may be a valuable exercise to examine every public communication and ask, "Which of the Shaping Virtues are we modeling for our people?" When we speak publicly, we are modeling something for our people.

James Clear adapted the famous adage, "Rome wasn't built in a day, but they were laying bricks every hour."[40] What was true for Rome is true for our churches. Our people are always watching, studying, and learning from our examples, growling and all. If we rush to try and slap on these virtues all at once, people will be confused, overwhelmed, and disoriented. But if we lay shaping-virtues bricks one at a time in each personal and public interaction, we will build something of lasting import.

---

[40] James Clear, "Rome Wasn't Built in a Day, But They Were Laying Bricks Every Hour." https://jamesclear.com/lay-a-brick

10

THE ROLE OF OUR SHAPING VIRTUES IN GLOBAL PARTNERSHIP

Dave Taylor

Lead Pastor, Sovereign Grace Church (Sydney, Australia)

M y very first interaction with Sovereign Grace Churches came in 1995 when a pastor named C.J. Mahaney came to visit my church in the UK. I still remember it so very well. He spoke on "Christ and Him Crucified" and it was immediately evident that this man really loved the Savior. I'd never seen a man cry while he was preaching before. He was so grateful for what Jesus had done for him and so captivated by it; he simply couldn't help it. I wanted to love Jesus like that, and yet what blew me away even more, was what took place after the service had concluded.

A Personal Testimony

I was 19 years old at the time and well used to having senior leaders come into town. They always wore a suit and tie, came in right as the service was about to start and then usually headed off very quickly afterwards. If there was time for a conversation, then that'd only be done with other senior leaders and important folk. This was the norm I was used to after many years

Yet this guy, C.J. Mahaney, was different from that. For a start, he looked different. There was no suit and tie in sight! But more than that, as soon as the service concluded, he stayed around just chatting with people. He wanted to get to know the church, the individuals in the church. Then I watched as he made his way outside. He picked up a soccer ball and proceeded to play ball with some of the kids. It's a simple thing. To many, it would've been no big deal at all. For me, though, given what I was used to, it simply blew me away.

What I was witnessing that day is called humility, and the more I got to see C.J. Mahaney as well as so many other leaders in Sovereign Grace, the more I got to see that this humility wasn't an isolated trait. It was joined by other virtues like joy, gratitude, encouragement, generosity, servanthood, and godliness. All of the leaders I met at that time deeply loved Jesus. Gospel fruit was so evident in their lives, and I was sold. This is exactly what I wanted for my life. I wanted to know and love Jesus like they do. Therefore, I wonderfully found my home in Sovereign Grace.

The Testimony of Others

Now, some 27 years on, as I travel around the world on behalf of Sovereign Grace Churches, I have been privileged on so many different occasions to discover that there's plenty more stories out there just like mine. Pastors who at some point have come across Sovereign Grace, maybe through a song or a friend, and who have then gone on to listen to some of our messages and read our books.

They've been greatly affected by our music and our writing and our teaching, wanting to know more. But when they've actually started to encounter some of our people, either through pastoral visits or at a conference, they've been blown away. They've encountered a culture marked by humility, joy, gratitude, encouragement, generosity, servanthood and godliness. At that point, they want nothing else, just like it was for me.

We are certainly not the only denomination to enjoy these virtues. I have no doubt that there are many more out there, and thank God for that. But within Sovereign Grace Churches, the pursuit of these Shaping Virtues are a priority; they matter dearly to us. These virtues aren't optional extras, something to either take or leave. Rather, they're important markers of who we really are, flowing out of the gospel that we love. They're part of our culture in Sovereign Grace, and part of our mission not just locally, but globally as well.

Virtues and Mission

For that reason, these virtues over many years now, have been playing a very important role in our work of planting and strengthening churches around the world. At the time of this printing, we have the privilege of working into 39 different nations outside of the United States. We are increasingly becoming a global family of churches. As such, we continue to move forward eagerly desiring to make ensure these Shaping Virtues mark our gospel culture around the world.

To that end, whenever we plant a Sovereign Grace Church around the world, we want to plant with pastors that are gospel saturated and, as a result, who model these virtues for the dear saints that are entrusted to their care. We want to plant with pastors who simply can't help themselves, since they're so personally affected by the gospel.

That's why the Pastors College is so important, not only the United States college, but indeed all of our colleges around the world. These colleges, I believe, play an important role in teaching a pastor to watch his life and doctrine closely. This includes the embodiment of these shaping, gospel-saturated values. Because planters are ambassadors of both Jesus Christ and of Sovereign Grace in a new country or culture, it's important that we plant with men and teams that truly embody gospel culture.

Beyond planting churches, these Shaping Virtues play a very important role as we explore new global partnerships for Sovereign Grace Churches. When pastors reach out to us from the various corners of the world, one of the important items we consider is compatibility. We are not interested in accumulating churches for the sake of growth, but in building with churches who believe and cherish the same things we do.

To this end, we always begin with what we believe, our Statement of Faith and our Seven Shared Values. We also talk through and seek to look for compatibility with our Shaping Virtues: How has the gospel shaped the culture of their church? Are we on the same page when it comes to what the gospel produces? And are we saturated and affected by the same things?

This sometimes leads to an end of the pursuit of partnership, and we're okay with that. Again, our goal is not growth for growth's sake, but to discover where the Lord is joining us with like-minded gospel-partners, that we might faithfully labor together for His glory. And it is a sweet and glorious moment when we find churches who are keen to be a part of us and share in our beliefs in doctrine and in culture. In God's kindness, I've experienced this many times. And, by his grace, I don't believe we're done yet.

As we labor around the world to plant and partner with churches, my hope and prayer is that these Shaping Virtues will remain important, cherished, and present traits of whatever God gives us the grace to build. They've wonderfully marked who we are for many years. As we continue to move forward around the world, I pray they'll mark us for many years to come.

11

SHAPING VIRTUES AMONG THE SHEPHERDS

Jon Payne
Senior Pastor, Redemption Hill Church (Round Rock, TX)

> *By this all people will know that you are my disciples,*
> *if you have love for one another. (John 13:35)*

S ince pastors have written this journal focused on SGC's "Shaping Virtues," one might expect wise and wide-ranging instruction and application of these gospel-shaped virtues to our churches and the people we serve. However, it's possible for us as pastors to do all that while failing to make sufficient application to ourselves. Perhaps even more subtly, to fail to make sufficient application to our pastoral teams.

Sinful Tendencies

Perhaps you can identify with one, some or all of the following statements. I've been impatient when fellow pastors wanted to extend a pastoral discussion. I've been proud when fellow pastors pointed out ways I could grow. I've been jealous when other pastors received attention that I wanted. I've been lazy when other pastors needed my diligence. I've allowed self-righteous thoughts to linger toward other pastors' sins. I've lacked compassion toward other pastors' weaknesses. I've judged other pastors' motives.

These sins aren't constant and thankfully, so far, have not been excessive or disqualifying. They are present, however. Perhaps, on many occasions, my fellow pastors were not aware of these sinful urges in my heart. But the Lord saw. The Lord knew. What a miracle the Lord is merciful and gracious, slow to anger and abounding in steadfast love. And what a mercy to pastor alongside merciful pastors as well.

These sinful tendencies should concern us because we know that the effect of sin, all sin, is the dishonoring of the Lord. When left unchecked, the sins of pastors dishonor the Lord, directly resulting in the church being tempted and its health and effectiveness undermined. A pastoral team that preaches the gospel but fails to allow it to shape its relationships is daring sin to undermine all of its other pastoral labors for the church. This happens when sin festers in the soul of a pastoral team and poisons the gospel-shaped character that ought to be modeled before the church.

The final explosion of this neglect often takes place in nasty church splits, divided pastoral teams, or at least undesired departures. Less severe consequences include the ineffectiveness of the team in leading the church. Pastors cannot be very effective in watching over the flock if they're angry at each other!

Pastors Need Gospel Application

Sometimes pastors are so focused on caring for the rest of the flock and the welfare of the church that we neglect to apply the gospel to our interactions with the pastoral team. We mean well in our efforts to serve. However, neglecting gospel relationships and conduct on our pastoral teams is misguided and dangerous. Caring for the church and caring for the team are not opposing goals; they are necessary friends. It serves the church for the pastoral team to cultivate gospel character toward each other.

Other times, we deny the need for godly virtue altogether, settling for an attempt at mere external politeness among the pastoral team. We are not called to niceness, but to love. And love, the summary and highpoint of all gospel virtues, only comes as we bring our imperfect selves to the gospel we teach to others.

Pastors need gospel application in those unsanctified parts of our heart as we interact with our fellow pastors. We need "church office" gospel application, "elder meeting" gospel application, "Sunday review" gospel application, "job review" gospel application, "role transition" gospel application, "budget planning" gospel application, and "decision disagreement" gospel application. We need the Shaping Virtues of the gospel among the shepherds.

Philippians 1:27 ought to inform our pastoral relationships. "Let your manner of life be worthy of the gospel of Christ…" In other words, make sure gospel virtues are abounding among the shepherds.

A Few Scenarios

Here are a few practical scenarios that come to mind, where these seven Shaping Virtues ought to be applied.

Humilty

A fellow pastor shares an observation about your recent message or ministry event. Our pride rushes to our defense, demanding that we be honored. But humility remembers that our reputation is found in Christ. We want to receive the input of our fellow pastors so that we can show progress in our ministry and serve the flock well.

Joy

The pastoral team is discouraged because of a recent membership departure. The burdens of ministry weigh heavy on our hearts. However, each team member can model joy for their brothers as they recount and remember God's grace and faithfulness. Joy is a gospel virtue that we can give on a regular basis to our fellow pastors in the long and tiring journey of pastoring.

Gratitude

A fellow pastor has been behind in his assignments recently and has caused some burdens for his fellow pastors. The natural response is self-righteousness and grumbling. If not out loud, we at least do this in our heart (and perhaps when we get home). But the gratitude that flows from our own experience of God's mercy causes us to consider the many ways that God has been kind to us through this brother. Recounting those gifts will cause our gratefulness for him to overwhelm our temptation to complain.

Encouragement

A pastor is sharing some struggles in his marriage and parenting. A misguided and too-busy fellow pastor might make the assumption that pastors don't need spiritual encouragement. But the gospel transforms our mouths into fountains of living water that are meant to refresh our fellow brothers. The church only grows as we speak the truth of God's life-giving Word to each other. This is true for pastors, too. Gospel-drenched encouragement must be prioritized among the shepherds.

Generosity

A pastor on the team has just had a baby or an illness in the family or is moving to a new home. Mere colleagues may offer congratulations or sympathy, but generous pastors will look for ways to give of themselves to help their fellow pastors. Generosity may also come into play in the very practical consideration of pastoral compensation or the annual budget discussion. Generous pastors are not looking to protect their own position or their ministry budgets at the expense of their fellow pastors but to be generous personally and in ministry in how they relate to their brothers.

Servanthood

An unpleasant pastoral need has come to the attention of the whole team. Perhaps it is a difficult counseling conversation, a tedious administrative task, or a thankless job that simply has to be done. A selfish pastor looks to avoid difficult pastoral assignments. A servant-hearted team views those moments as opportunities to love one another. As the Lord washed the feet of his disciples, so we ought to wash one another's feet.

Godliness

The needs of the church multiply and sometimes pastors neglect the growth of their own soul. But a team devoted to sanctification will take time to spur each other on toward godliness. A godly team keeps watch over the souls of their fellow pastors: their devotional life, their marriage, their parenting, their growth in grace. These areas are not sacrificed to serve the development of the church. How easy for pastoral teams to assume godliness and accent ministry. Let it not be so among us. Let us emphasize godliness and trust the Lord for the growth of our ministry.

A Final Appeal

In all of these scenarios, and countless others, my appeal is that we allow the gospel-informed Shaping Virtues to shape our character toward our fellow pastors. We must keep watch over our own souls, including the soul of our pastoral team, lest we malign the gospel ministry with character unworthy of the gospel. Let our teams of shepherds be shaped by the gospel of the Chief Shepherd.

12

SHAPING VIRTUES IN SMALL GROUP

Andy Farmer

Elder, Covenant Fellowship Church (Glen Mills, PA)

For nearly four decades I've been attending small groups in my local church. If I do the math on the number of small group meetings I've attended over those years I arrive at a conservative estimate of over five hundred meetings. That's a lot of grouping! When I first started, small groups were the cool thing churches were doing. Showing up at Alan and Linda Redrup's house was a highlight of our week. We weren't always the first to arrive but we definitely staked our claim as the last to leave.

You go to enough small groups over time and you discover that not all small group experiences are life changing. There are times I've wondered, "What are we doing here?" That's even happened in groups I've been leading! But over the years I've learned a huge lesson. The gathering of the church, whether it is all together or "breaking bread in their homes" (Acts 2:46), is not for the purpose of epic experience. That can happen at particular moments. (I can point to some key small group meetings that were life changing for me.) However, small groups don't accomplish their main purpose that way.

Shaped Over Time

Small groups shape us over time. In the words of the Apostle Paul, they help us

> grow up in every way into him who is the head, into Christ, from whom the whole body, joined and held together by every joint with which it is equipped, when each part is working properly, makes the body grow so that it builds itself up in love (Eph. 4:15–16).

There is nothing in Paul's language that says we can grow up in Christ alone. We grow as we are joined and held together as a body. There is also nothing that says we can grow up in a single event. The whole flow of Paul's words is about experience over time. Finally, there is no lack of clarity about the goal of our growing together. It is to build up the body in love, into Christ. A small group is healthy when all of its members are meaningfully connected, relating toward a common goal, over time, becoming more like Christ.

So how do we know whether a group is, over time, actually promoting this healthy life together? Our Shaping Virtues can provide a wonderful guide to making sure our small group is accomplishing the purpose for which it is intended.

Humility

We find a wonderful sense of commonality when we come into our small group aware that we are needy—"works in progress"—and we simply let people see us that way. If you've ever been in a business or committee meeting where everyone is trading on their strengths and skills, you know what competition for first importance is all about. But if we humbly acknowledge to each other what we all know to be true about ourselves, we find our focus shifts from our position in the group to God's grace working through the group (Jas. 4:6).

Joy and Gratitude

More times than I'd like to admit I look at small group night on my calendar and secretly hope there is a city-wide electrical outage that cancels our group but keeps my TV working at home. But it really isn't hard to access joy as I get my lazy self up to go. I can remember the joy of my early years as a Christian, when gathering together with the saints was new and delightful. I can think of those saints in other places where gathering is not permitted, or in our own country where gathering isn't easy. And I can remind myself of how God has given me some of my closest relationships through attending the same small group together.

Mostly I can access joy to attend because joy is both a gift of salvation and the meaningful response to finding myself a child of God through the saving work of Christ. In other words, joy and gratitude are intertwined. As I consider what God has done for me on the cross and is doing with me in his church my heart wells with gratitude and a real joy motivates me toward my small group.

Encouragement

This is one of the greatest aspects of a healthy small group experience. We gather together and 'come alongside' one another; that's the literal idea behind encouragement. We encourage folks who are in the battle with sin and the world. We comfort one another in times of trial and remind each other of how God loves us. I tell my community group leaders, they can drop a lot of balls and swing and miss in their discussion in a group or meeting, but a group that learns to encourage one another is a place people want to be.

Generosity

This is where I've seen God move mightily through groups. Even now I know folks in our church who would be destitute without the financial and practical help they are getting from their friends. One group I oversaw a few years ago went so far in its generosity toward a member battling cancer that its effort was noted in *USA Today*. A group doesn't have to have deep pockets either. Often times what is most meaningful to people is not lavish provision, but timely support—paying for a car repair, covering a rent payment, providing an anonymous gift card for a family outing. People don't need to know who is being generous, they just need to experience generosity.

Servanthood

Servanthood flows out of the others-focused practice that small groups train us in. It comes in the form of wise counsel, compassionate prayer, and careful conversation. But it also comes in the more practical forms of helping move, providing meals or babysitting. The key here is mutuality. We may be the one who serves at one point, but eventually we will need to receive service ourselves. What a wonderful thing to sit in a group knowing that all of the members have been on both sides of that equation with each other at some point.

Godliness

This brings us back full circle. The goal of small group is to "grow up in every way into him … into Christ" (Eph. 4:15). That's a great definition of godliness: growing into Christ. It is a process that won't be completed until we are glorified in the age to come, but it is something we should be experiencing throughout our lives. Our lives are meant to rub against each other to form something we can't be by ourselves: distinctive representatives of Jesus Christ to a desperate world.

Helping One Another Along the Journey

Small groups are a place where God works in us together so that we can see him work through us to others. I love the way John Loftness says it in the book that carved out SGC's vision for gathering together in homes. In *Why Small Groups?* he says,

> We're like the Israelites trudging through the wilderness, like the disciples huddled in the upper room after Jesus' ascension, like the pilgrims on the Mayflower. The negative view is that we're stuck with one another— confined by a desert, a hostile Jerusalem, or a stormy sea. But 'stuck' is not the biblical attitude. Rather, we belong to

one another. We are pilgrims on our way to the promised land, called to help one another along on the journey.[41]

We help one another as we manifest the very Shaping Virtues we've listed above. When a group is marked by those, small group has depth, purpose, and meaning. And that is why small groups exist.

[41] John Loftness, *Why Small Groups?*, ed. C.J. Mahaney (Gaithersburg, MD: People of Destiny International, 1996), 23.

13

SHAPING VIRTUES IN THE HOME

Aaron Mayfield

Elder, Redemption Hill Church (Round Rock, TX)

Once when preaching a sermon to our young church plant, my 5-year-old son decided to flip upside down on his chair and make faces at me. My wife was out of town, and I had no way to reach him without calling more attention to the scene. It was one of those moments nobody prepared me for as a parent.

For about 3 seconds I thought, "I can handle this." Then one of the other moms decided to draw even more attention to my little gymnast by walking to the front of the church so she could get photographic evidence of his joyful performance. The entire church was then captivated by the fruit of my parenting on full display!

As the father of five sons, I was pretty surprised to receive an invitation to write on the topic of parenting. Our house is loud. It is very loud. We have a punch card at all the local emergency rooms. (We are almost at 10% off our next visit!) Moments like the one I described above usually leave me resolved not to write on parenting any time soon.

And yet, our home is full of life. It is full of laughter. My wife and I continually strive to have a home characterized by joy and gratitude. So while we are still learning, we ask ourselves regularly, "How can we cultivate joy? How do we nurture virtue? How might we foster an atmosphere that promotes growth in Christ-likeness?" These questions are really just different ways of asking, "How can we make sure we're applying the gospel in our home?"

The Compelling Attraction of a Life Shaped by Christian Virtue

Sovereign Grace Churches has long prioritized the deep work of sanctification in the life of the believer. We have a heritage of family discipleship. And it was this trait that drew me and my wife to join this family of churches almost 20 years ago.

The Lord calls us to live lives worthy of the gospel (Eph. 4:1, Phil. 1:27, etc), and to make every effort to supplement our faith with virtue (2 Pet. 1:5). This results in men and women, young and old, who bear the fruit of hearts nourished with the life-giving effects of the gospel.

The character of our marriages and the fruit of our parenting are a telling story of the effect of what we believe. To say that more positively, when our home life is shaped by Christian virtue we present a compelling attraction to a world that is spinning out of control.

Cultivating Homes Shaped by Christian Virtue

We have a wonderful opportunity as spouses and parents to cultivate Christian virtue in our homes. I love how the Dutch reformer, Herman Bavinck, puts it in his book on the Christian family:

> Everything in the home contributes to nurture—the hand of the father, the voice of the mother, the older brother, the younger sister, the infant in the bassinet, the sickly sibling, grandmother and grandchildren, uncles and aunts, guests and friends, prosperity and adversity, celebrations and mourning, Sundays and workdays, prayers and thanksgiving at mealtime and the reading of God's Word, morning devotions and evening devotions. Everything is serviceable for nurturing each other day by day, hour by hour, without plan, without appointment, without technique, all of which are set beforehand. Everything possesses power to nurture, apart from being able to analyze and calculate that power... The family is the school of life, because it is the fountain and hearth of life.[42]

Do you see what he's suggesting here? We are to see everything in our homes as a potential instrument to nurturing faith. The home is full of moments and relationships in which these Shaping Virtues can be cultivated. Mealtimes and bedtimes and everything in between present daily opportunities to instill these virtues and enjoy the fruit thereof.

---

[42] Herman Bavinck, *The Christian Family* (Grand Rapids, MI: Christian's Library Press, 2012), 106–107.

The virtues aren't an end in themselves. They flow from hearts set on understanding and applying the gospel. This means we celebrate the gospel together as a family in the morning time. When we sit together at meals, we want to discuss the reasons that Jesus came.[43] When conflicts occur, we want to be quick to look to the cross as the lens through which we view one another and the wrongs committed.

Our marriages can be appropriately marked by humility because we are aware that we are fellow sinners ransomed by the blood of Christ. Encouragement will flow naturally because we spend time training our kids to identify evidences of God's grace at work in one another's lives. Gratitude should be commonplace as we recognize that we have not been treated as we deserve, and we rightly respond in thanksgiving. Generosity ought to be a regular theme because we love to reflect our generous God.

It starts with us as parents. Do we let these Shaping Virtues inform our approach to our relationships at home? When the gospel is rightly understood, when it takes hold in our hearts, it will produce the fruit of Christian virtue in our lives.

Celebrating the Virtues in Our Homes

One specific way to cultivate these Shaping Virtues in our homes is by celebrating them when we see them displayed in each other's lives. As spouses and parents, we should make it a goal to catch one another doing good, outdoing one another in showing honor (Rom. 12:10).

---

[43] See John Piper's excellent book, *Fifty Reasons Why Jesus Came to Die*

What do you celebrate in your home? What do you make a big deal out of? Is it achievement? Is it high test scores? Perhaps it's victories on the sports field?

As we saw earlier in this journal, these virtues are both commanded and modeled in Scripture, supremely by Jesus himself. As we encourage one another in Christ-likeness, we should become skilled at seeing these virtues working themselves out in the lives of our spouse and kids. Make a big deal out of those moments when your teenager serves one of his siblings. When your 8-year-old expresses gratitude, that's a moment to commend him. As you see your weary spouse fighting for joy in the midst of a difficult season, point out how that is God at work in their life.

Consider even having a special celebratory dinner when you catch one of your kids demonstrating the fruit of these virtues in their life. Be creative and intentional in how you celebrate God's work in your home because in doing so you are ultimately glorifying him who is at work completing the work he has begun (Phil. 1:6).

And when you fail, again, look to Christ who forgives your sin and displays his power in your weakness. Remember these too are moments where we are able to enjoy and model the virtues of humility and joy in Christ, not in our performance. And don't miss the moment to demonstrate grace in repentance and forgiveness. God gives grace to the humble (Jas. 4:6)!

So realize the great adventure it is to cultivate and celebrate these virtues in the home. Train your kids up in the way they should go. Consider taking a single virtue and spending a week's worth of dinner conversations talking about the scriptural emphasis. Identify and celebrate where you see that virtue at work in your spouse and children. And as you do this slow and steady work, be prepared for our good and faithful God to bear wonderful fruit in your home.

14

SHAPING VIRTUES IN GRANDPARENTING

Larry McCall

Elder, Christ's Covenant Church (Winona Lake, IN)

H ere is a heart-searching exercise. Imagine that you have passed away, and the pastor presiding at your funeral asks your now-adult grandchildren to give a testimony at your memorial service of the impact you had on their lives. What will your grandchildren say at your funeral? What do you hope they will say?

Leaving a Legacy

As grandparents, we want to make a difference in the lives of our grandchildren—a lasting difference—the kind of difference that will last into eternity. We want to leave a legacy not just of money or things, but a legacy of faith, a legacy of love and dependence on Jesus, a legacy of lives marked by the Shaping Virtues of humility, joy, generosity, and gratitude.

So, how does that happen? What would have to be true of our lives as grandparents to make a Christ-honoring, eternal impact on our grandchildren?

The Apostle Paul drew attention specifically to the powerful legacy of a godly grandmother when he wrote to his closest protégé. At the beginning of 2 Timothy, Paul reflected, "I am reminded of your sincere faith, a faith that dwelt first in your grandmother Lois and your mother Eunice and now, I am sure, dwells in you as well" (2 Tim. 1:5). The apostle was clearly honoring the impact that Timothy's godly grandmother and mother had in his life, acknowledging God's grace at work in the transmission of a life of faith from one generation to the next. Isn't that the implication of Paul's exhortation to Timothy a bit later in the letter?

> But as for you, continue in what you have learned and have firmly believed, knowing *from whom* you learned it and how from childhood you have been acquainted with the sacred writings, which are able to make you wise for salvation through faith in Christ Jesus (2 Tim. 3:14–15, emphasis mine).

Paul was reminding Timothy not only of the words of life he had learned as a boy growing up, but he was also drawing Timothy's recollection back to the people from whom Timothy had learned the gospel—including his own godly grandmother. God had used the gospel teaching of a godly grandmother, given increased impact by her gospel-reflecting example, in shaping the life of young Timothy, a man used greatly by God in the spread of the gospel. Now, that's a legacy worth investing in as grandparents, the legacy of a godly life example.

As we grandparents pursue Christ with gospel-motivated passion, what fruit of the gospel should we be praying for in our own everyday lives? We should be praying for fruit that will serve as a Christ-reflecting legacy for our grandchildren.

Grandfathers and Grandmothers

Spending some time in Titus 2 may be helpful. How does Titus 2 begin? "But as for you [Pastor Titus], teach what accords with sound doctrine" (Titus 2:1). Teaching the content of "sound doctrine," the truths of the gospel of Jesus Christ as they are delineated in Titus 3:4–7, is necessary for every healthy church. But this sound doctrine, this gospel truth, must not be left hanging in some detached, ethereal form. It must be applied very practically to the daily lives of the members of the churches. So, Titus is charged by the apostle to teach "what accords with" sound doctrine. It is as if Paul is writing, "Show the believers what difference the gospel makes in their everyday lives. Help the believers live out the gospel 'so that in everything they may adorn the doctrine of God our Savior' " (Titus 2:10). Then, Paul describes what the everyday life of Christians should look like in various life situations when fueled by the gospel of Jesus Christ.

For the sake of this article, let's start with grandfathers. What God-honoring, Christ-reflecting, gospel-fueled character traits should be evident in the lives of older men? Paul says that "Older men are to be sober-minded, dignified, self-controlled, sound in faith, in love, and in steadfastness" (Titus 2:2). Rather than children seeing the older men in the church as "grumpy old men," ranting and raving about politics, the economy, the weather, they should grow up seeing the grandfathers in the church as faithful, joyful, gracious, loving servants of the Most High God. Why give them reasons to question the effectiveness of the gospel on everyday life? Older men, by God's grace, let us give our grandchildren a living example of the effects of God's gospel on our everyday lives.

What about grandmothers? Enabled by God's grace, what kind of legacy can Christian grandmothers leave for the coming generations? Let's look at Titus 2:3–4. "Older women likewise are to be reverent in behavior, not slanderers or slaves to much wine. They are to teach what is good, and so train the young women." Ladies, by God's grace, leave a life legacy that is marked by a daily awareness of God and his amazing mercy to you. May your life be marked by gospel-shaped gratitude that affects not only your attitudes but also your words as you pour into the coming generations the supremacy of Christ in the daily life of your family.

Empowered by Grace

So, what empowers this growth of character in the lives of grandparents? Is it a matter of mere determination? "Just do it?" Let's keep reading a bit longer in Titus 2. There's a connecting word in verse 11 that adds hope and help in this pursuit of leaving a godly life legacy. Do you see it? It's the word "for." After painting pictures of what the everyday lives of ordinary Christians in various life situations should look like, the apostle Paul adds these encouraging words about God's extraordinary gospel:

> For the grace of God has appeared, bringing salvation for all people, training us to renounce ungodliness and worldly passions, and to live self-controlled, upright, and godly lives in the present age (Titus 2:11-12).

Ordinary Christians can live extraordinary lives of godliness because they are empowered by God's extraordinary grace.

But, for grandparents to leave a contagious, godly impact on the coming generation, there needs to be intentional, meaningful time spent with the grandchildren. Though many grandparents in our culture are challenged with the hurdle of long-distance grandparenting, God in his mercy has let us live in an era in which we can have regular contact with our grandchildren even if they live far away. When we are with our grandchildren, personally or virtually, let us be intentional in letting them see the surpassing value of Christ in our lives. Are they hearing and seeing us live joyfully in a God-dependent, God-honoring way?

My fellow-grandparents, the way we live everyday life will leave a lasting impact on our grandchildren. That is what they will remember: not just our words, but the way we lived everyday life. That is what they will talk about at our funerals. Wouldn't it be wonderful if our adult grandchildren would say, "For my grandpa/grandma, to live was Christ and to die was gain"? Let's lean on the help of the Holy Spirit as we grandparents devote ourselves to continuing to grow in grace until that day when Christ calls us home. May our grandchildren see Christ in us, and may that leave a lasting impact on them.

15

SHAPING VIRTUES AND OUR WITNESS

Jim Donohue

Elder, Covenant Fellowship Church (Glen Mills, PA)

Years ago I was leading a Bible study with an eclectic group of new Christians as well as some non-Christians. The last study was on the importance of the local church. After the meeting, I wasn't sure where one of the participants stood with everything, so I asked, "Bill, are you planning on coming to church now that the Bible study is over?"

"It ain't gonna be that easy!" he responded.

When I asked him why, he simply replied, "Spring and all." Bill wasn't a farmer, so I am not sure what he was referring to, but it probably had to do with mulching and tending his yard.

"It ain't gonna be that easy" is a true assessment of many things that God calls us to, but it's especially true when it comes to reaching out to others with the message of the gospel. It ain't gonna be that easy because we live in a rapidly evolving, post-Christian world. Christian beliefs seem increasingly strange in a culture that doesn't understand our values. It's almost like we're living in a different universe. Our neighbors, co-workers, classmates, and family members don't know the Bible and don't understand the gospel. They don't see it as relevant to their lives. Some go further and view Christianity as a tool of oppression, with sharing the gospel qualifying as hate speech.

This is where our Shaping Virtues play a key role. They're meant to testify to the power of the gospel which has changed our lives.

Joy, Gratitude, Humility, and Service

Take joy for example. The world does not and cannot know the joy that we do. How could they? It's very difficult to experience true joy when this life is all there is. It's even harder when you don't have a relationship with Christ. Believers know the joy of being united to Christ, secure in his love, with eternity in front of us. Unbelievers should see the joy of Christ in our lives. When they do, they'll take note.

Consider gratitude. Most people aren't naturally very grateful. Complaining abounds in traffic, at work, and even in conversations about the weather or the preacher. It almost feels like ingratitude is a "shaping virtue" in our culture. This should not be the case with Christians. We should be the most thankful people on the planet. Do you express gratitude when you're chatting with a co-worker or talking to a neighbor? Or do you instead complain? Gratitude to God is counter-cultural and a powerful way to demonstrate the difference Christ has made in our lives.

One of the rarest virtues we can embody is humility. The message of the gospel is infinitely important, but how we say it can affect whether someone hears us or not. Humility should mark our interactions with others, just like it did for Jesus. When we listen well, ask good questions, and respect those we're talking to, we show people what Christ is like. In a world that has thrown listening and respect out the window, let's be known for demonstrating humility, even when it's not being demonstrated to us.

Our differences with others don't need to be hindrances. They can shine forth the light of Christ! Let's say you have a neighbor you want to reach out to but you don't know how. Maybe they seem a little intimidating or unfriendly, or maybe you're afraid that they will reject you. What should you do? Try looking for ways to serve them: make a meal, watch their dog, or mow their lawn when they're away.

During the pandemic, my family and I helped our neighbors build a new deck on the back of their house. We were all trapped at home anyway, so it was a perfect time to do something like this. Our time together forged a strong relationship with them. A week after we finished, they had us over (on their new deck) for a thank you dinner. They said what we did was the nicest thing that anyone had ever done for them. It wasn't that big of a sacrifice for us, but it meant the world to them. If our goal is to show people the power of the gospel, then let's show them the servant heart of Christ by finding meaningful ways to serve them.

The Corporate Witness of the Church

Shaping Virtues are essential for us as individual followers of Christ sharing his love with others. But the reality is that our co-workers and neighbors can write off one person or family as an exception. They can see your joy as a rare personality trait. They can chalk up your thankfulness to a good upbringing. But when they see an entire church that is full of joy, when they meet other believers who are filled with thankfulness, they can't write you off anymore.

Sociologists have coined the phrase, "plausibility structures" which determine for people whether a story is believable or unbelievable. The main factor determining our plausibility structures isn't evidence or experience, but rather the communities that we interact with. Sam Chan says:

> One of the major reasons our friends aren't Christians is that they don't belong to a community of friends who also believe in Jesus. It's not primarily because they haven't heard the gospel (they probably haven't, but they already think they know what you believe). It's not because there's not enough evidence for the Christian faith (because no matter how much evidence you produce, they'll explain it away). In many cases, the number one reason our friends aren't Christians is that they don't have any other Christian friends.[44]

---

[44] Sam Chan, *How to Talk about Jesus (without Being That Guy)* (Grand Rapids, MI: Zondervan, 2020), 8.

This is exactly why an important part of our outreach strategy is building friendships with non-Christians, But we do not do it just one-on-one. Bringing our unbelieving friends into our network of friendships is one of the best things we can do because it adjusts their plausibility structures. It enables them to think differently about the relevance and truth of the gospel. This is what we call our corporate witness. Together, as the church, we live out our shaping virtues and testify to the truth and power of Christ which has changed our lives.

Acts 2:42–47 shows us the power of a strong corporate witness:

> And they devoted themselves to the apostles' teaching and the fellowship, to the breaking of bread and the prayers. And awe came upon every soul, and many wonders and signs were being done through the apostles. And all who believed were together and had all things in common. And they were selling their possessions and belongings and distributing the proceeds to all, as any had need. And day by day, attending the temple together and breaking bread in their homes, they received their food with glad and generous hearts, praising God and having favor with all the people. And the Lord added to their number day by day those who were being saved.

Displaying the Power of the Gospel

Like we see in the early church, virtues have a direct connection to witness. The early church was shockingly different from the culture around them. When the Holy Spirit filled them, they immediately became devoted to the church and the teaching of

God's Word. They joined their lives together in deep fellowship, eating together and praying together and sharing life together. They were also extraordinarily generous, sharing everything they had and even selling their possessions to give to each other. These changes, these differences, showed the watching world the power of the gospel. Their love for one another made the world sit up and take notice.

The same is true for us. Our virtues are directly connected to our witness. When non-Christians see biblical virtues and godly character in our lives and our church, how could they not take notice?

Our church runs an introduction to Christianity class called The Bridge Course, and many of our church members serve in different roles: group leaders and assistants, kitchen staff and administrators, childcare workers and greeters. Guests often comment about the way we care for one another as we work together. They see the deep bonds we have for one another and it makes a loud statement. It's not unusual for someone serving in The Bridge Course to be returning Tupperware from a shared meal, greeting a friend with a hug, or giving someone a ride. This mutual care provides a powerful witness to the watching world.

The care extends to our guests as well. Toward the end of the course, we attend an overnight retreat. It's not cheap, so to make sure our guests join us, we provide scholarships for whoever needs them. I tell our guests that the members of our church, most of whom they have never met, give generously so they can attend the retreat even if they can't pay a dime. Generosity like this is a clear demonstration of the generosity of God toward us.

Jesus said, "By this all people will know that you are my disciples, if you have love for one another" (John 13:35). Let's be a people that not only love the lost, but also love one another so that those around us might see a visible demonstration of the power of the gospel that has transformed our lives.

RECOMMENDED READING

"In a world so easily satisfied with images, it's too easy to waste our lives watching mindless television and squandering our free time away with entertainment. We have a higher calling. God has called us to live our lives by faith and not by sight—and this can mean nothing less than committing our lives to the pursuit of language, revelation, and great books."

TONY REINKE

1

HUMILITY: TRUE GREATNESS

By C. J. MAHANEY

Pete Payne

Pastor, Grace Community Church (Warminster, CO)

The Shaping Virtue of Humility

OUR WORLD HAS ESSENTIALLY determined that how we feel about ourselves at any given moment is of the utmost importance. From that perspective, I have done an extremely stupid thing. I volunteered to write a recommendation for C.J. Mahaney's book, *Humility: True Greatness.*

At first, I was looking forward to revisiting the book, in preparation for this assignment. I thought it would be humble of me to rely not on my memory, but instead on a fresh reading. That would best position me to exhort the spiritually younger and less humble to read in order to be helped, as I have been, by C.J.'s writing. Bad idea, for a number of reasons.

Humility is one of those biblically-defined constructs, like love, which has been significantly targeted for distortion by the combined forces of the world, the flesh, and the devil. Sadly, humility has come to be the attribute that everyone pretends to respect, but no one really wants (like Miss Congeniality at a beauty contest, or Most Sportsmanlike at an athletic awards dinner). Humility focuses on the good of others and is therefore intended only for losers. In a world dominated by feeling good about me, no one truly feels good about being 'a humble man with much to be humble about.'[45]

In re-reading *Humility*, I was reminded of why I love C.J.'s teaching and the richly theological and intensely practical aspects of his life and ministry. When my children were young, our family traveled to annual Celebration conferences. I was always amazed that my elementary-aged children not only could remember C.J.'s messages, but also could understand the takeaways, as well. Somehow, during the same messages, I was being challenged and instructed as a husband, father, and pastor.

So it is with *Humility*. This is a book that can be studied effectively by parents with their children. "Humility is our greatest friend; pride our greatest enemy." It is a book that does not cast the concept of humility on the trash heap of human philosophy, but defines it biblically. It is a book that exhorts each of us to examine our lives to see if this precious attribute, one that draws the attention and esteem of God, himself, is present and increasing. It is a book that holds out God's promise of true greatness through genuine servanthood. And it is a book, most significantly, that

---

[45] Attributed to Winston Churchill

points us to the greatest example of humility—the Lord Jesus Christ—and advocates that while we must emulate his example, we cannot do so until we have been ransomed and transformed by the quintessential demonstration of humility, his death on a cross.

I have been a believer for nearly 6 decades and involved in ministry leadership for more than half of that, but in re-reading this book, I was freshly convicted of my pride and regretful that I had not made a habit of taking the time to read this book on an annual basis. C.J. pointed me to Jesus; he directed me to the Word of God; he introduced me to his current and historical friends who through their writings had instructed him in the beauty and promise of humility as presented in Scripture. In his inimitable manner, he also reminded me of many wonderful and practical habits, rooted in the "whys" of Scripture, helping me to refocus on the path to true greatness, so often obscured by the enemies of my soul—world, flesh, and devil. He reminded me, as always, that it is not the hearers or even knowers of the Word, but the "doers" who will ultimately be found to be humble in the sight of God.

Humility: True Greatness is rich exhortation from a true, biblical friend, who longs for us all to join him as he endeavors to work out his salvation with the godly fear and trembling that is characteristic of genuine humility. If you have never read it, please move it to the top of your reading list. If you have read it before, read it again, trusting that God opposes the proud, but gives grace to the humble.

2

HAPPINESS

By RANDY ALCORN

Leo Parris

Pastor, Covenant Fellowship Church (Glen Mills, PA)

The Shaping Virtue of Joy

"AM I HAPPY?" IS the question that occupies much of our thoughts. Maybe, like me, you've asked yourself, "Is that okay? Does God want me to be happy?"

Wolves in sheep's clothing have built ministries off promises of happiness. To make matters worse, we sometimes feel our own joy oscillate as a litmus of the strength of our own idolatry.

All of this can cause me to be a wee bit skeptical toward promises of happiness. Instead of expecting happiness, I resign myself to an unflappable joy that is less emotional. I've even felt a pang of guilt at times for enjoying life thinking, "I must not be holy or serious enough!" But what does God's Word actually teach about happiness?

As I've studied this theme in Scripture, no resource proved more helpful than Randy Alcorn's *Happiness*. In accessible and plain style, its 400+ pages examine the main words for happiness in Scripture, how they relate, and how that ought to affect our pursuit of God.

In Part I, he lays out the central findings of his study. He establishes that longing for happiness is human and satisfied in God alone. It is a part of true spirituality, yet twisted by idolatry. God does want us to be happy and joyful, to experience a full-bodied gladness that flows from him and overflows in gratitude and produces holiness in us. Yet he's designed us to experience it in Christ.

In the second part, Alcorn examines God's happiness in his Triune relationships and in the incarnation of Christ. He shows that the Bible regularly speaks to the happiness (blessedness) of God. Take for example Paul's description in 1 Timothy 6:15, "God . . . in eternal felicity alone holds sway. He is King of kings and Lord of lords" (NEB). Our God is a happy God. That may sound trite, but when we consider that God himself is happy, it transforms our own happiness from something that is suspect to something he generously shares with us.

Part III contains potentially the most helpful section of the book. Here, he examines the Bible's words for happiness, yielding over 2,000 occurrences of synonyms. Alcorn helpfully explains why blessed is often chosen by translators over happiness and convincingly argues that these are to be treated as synonyms. A clear and compelling study of the biblical words asher, samach, markarios, chara, and chairō leads to the overwhelming conclusion that happiness really matters to God!

Alcorn turns a corner in Part IV to address our experience of happiness. He delves into the Christian's pursuit of happiness through means such as prayer, the Word, and the cultivation of gratitude. This section is richly illustrative and very relevant for every day application.

Meditating on the themes of this book lifted higher my own expectations for happiness. As I read, I began to wonder at God's kindness, my enjoyment of creation and worship became more exuberant, my lament became more hopeful, and my delight became more firmly rooted in God.

I pray that you, too, are encouraged as you read that God strongly desires your happiness. And that he provides it in himself.

3

CHOOSING GRATITUDE: YOUR JOURNEY TO JOY

By NANCY DEMOSS WOLGEMUTH

Matt Gray

Pastor, Living Hope Church (Fayetteville, AR)

The Shaping Virtue of Gratitude

I'D LIKE FOR YOU to do something for me. Take your index and middle finger and place them on your neck. Do you feel a pulse? Good, then read this book!

Here's my point: while we can easily detect a pulse in our body, it is much more difficult to detect a pulse in our spiritual life. In her book, *Choosing Gratitude: Your Journey to Joy*, Nancy DeMoss Wolgemuth places the Bible's call for gratitude upon our soul and asks, "Do you feel a pulse?"

Taking Your Gratitude Pulse

Perhaps you're like me, coming into this study of gratitude, assuming that you have a pretty good handle on the discipline. If so, expect not to find a throbbing pulse but a weak and faint one.

Throughout the book, I flashed between two different experiences: inspiration and conviction. I felt inspired to live a more grateful life for the glory of God. And simultaneously, I felt conviction where I have failed to glorify God as I ought.

This book is written for anyone who desires to live a life of gratitude. And why shouldn't we want to be more grateful? After all, as Wolgemuth says, "Giving thanks is an indicator of our true heart condition. Those who have been made righteous by the grace of God will be thankful people" (67).

Grace-Motivated Gratitude

Wolgemuth's recommendations throughout are grace motivated, not guilt motivated. Her book is gospel-centered from cover to cover. Having expected this to be a book demanding a discipline, I found it surprisingly refreshing. It is designed to reflect God's heart toward us, not scolding us to be more thankful but envisioning and empowering us with divine power to do so.

Using the gospel as the primary means of motivation to live gratefully, Wolgemuth states the problem in this way:

> In response to our abounding guilt, God poured out
> super-abounding grace. Should it not follow, then, that
> super-abounding grace ought to be met by

super-duper-abounding gratitude? But does it? Is the gratitude that flows out of your life as abounding as the grace that has flowed into your life? Undeniable guilt, plus undeserved grace, should equal unbridled gratitude...I say we start by making it our goal to have a heart that's as grateful toward God as the abounding grace He has poured into our life (35).

Expressing Gratitude

This is a book that offers you life, not death. It offers joy, not condemnation. It is filled with both principles from God's Word and practices for life application. For example, chapter 6 is devoted to the ways in which we can be intentional about giving thanks to those who are deserving in our life. Wolgemuth says, "Gratitude is not the quiet game. It begs to be expressed, both to God and to others. 'Silent gratitude,' Gladys Berthe Stern said, 'isn't much use to anyone' " (98).

I loved this book! No, I'm grateful for it! And if you decide to read it, I know you will be too.

4

PRACTICING AFFIRMATION: GOD-CENTERED PRAISE OF THOSE WHO ARE NOT GOD

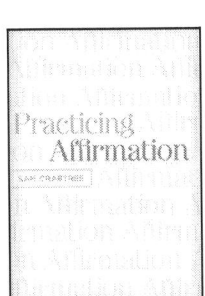

By SAM CRABTREE

Philip Estrada

Lead Pastor, Mission City Fellowship (San Antonio, TX)

The Shaping Virtue of Encouragement

THE BOOKS IS *Practicing Affirmation* by Sam Crabtree. John Piper describes it as "a healing balm for cranks, misfits, and malcontents who are so full of self they scarcely see, let alone celebrate, the simple beauties of imperfect virtue in others. Or to say it differently: I need this book."[46]

---

[46] From the Foreword.

Our beloved friend and pastor C.J. Mahaney gives a resounding affirmation of it when he says, "Too many of us use most of our words each day for criticizing and complaining. If you find that your communication lacks encouragement, if you want to grow in affirming others, if you plan to say any words at all today—please read this book!"[47]

I'm not the sharpest tool in the shed but when John Piper says "I need this book" and C.J. Mahaney says "Please read this book," I can take a hint. I should probably read this book!

What is Practicing Affirmation?

This book does more than simply help you to be a more encouraging person. Sam addresses affirmation as we typically understand it: puffing others up even if there really isn't much to puff up. Someone we know expresses a desire to be president and instead of responding with affirmation that still lives in the realm of reality, we choose to affirm him with "psyched-up positive thinking" (101). This is actually a broken understanding of affirmation and sadly, our affirmation often looks this way. Sam points this out among other affirmation pitfalls, in his chapter "Mistakes I Have Made."

Sam helps us see that affirmation doesn't begin when our kid hits a home run. Affirmation began at the point when God designed all of creation to affirm his glory. Affirmation as designed by God is not merely telling someone "good game." Instead, Sam helps us define biblical affirmation as being "God-centered, pointing to the image of God in a person." He expands on this by saying, "The only

---

[47] Back cover endorsement

commendable attributes in people were given to them. Everything is from God, through God, and to God so that in all things—including the commendable qualities in people—he might get the glory" (18).

Sam takes affirmation as we know it and unpacks it like the unwrapping of a priceless diamond that's been hidden away in some dirty old rag. You knew there was something good wrapped up there, but as it is revealed to you, it is far more beautiful than you had previously imagined. I feel that this is the effect Sam's helpful insight has had on my understanding of God-designed and God-centered affirmation.

Why Give Ourselves to Practicing Affirmation?

When we withhold affirmation or are simply not looking for it, we fail to recognize and commend the image of God in all people. Image bearers are mirroring the image of the God they were created to reflect, some as restored mirrors and some as broken mirrors. That means that in both the regenerate and unregenerate, there is something there for us to commend. Should we avoid this topic altogether, we are in danger of falling short of giving God the glory he deserves. We also can miss out on the good that is found in recognizing God's glory and work in people's lives.

God has prepared for us many means of grace through the giving and receiving of God-exalting affirmation. My marriage, parenting, pastoring, preaching, and life lived among my neighbors have been refreshed in the joy of Christ by growing in seeing God at work through the practice of affirmation. May this book serve you in the same way.

5

THE TREASURE PRINCIPLE: UNLOCKING THE SECRET OF JOYFUL GIVING

By RANDY ALCORN

Cedric Moss

Senior Pastor, Kingdom Life Church (Nassau, Bahamas)

The Shaping Virtue of Generosity

AS ONE WHO IS skeptical by nature, I generally question claims people make—especially big claims. A big claim I questioned is one made by Randy Alcorn in the opening pages of his small book, *The Treasure Principle*. Alcorn boldly asserts that "there's a fundamental connection between our spiritual lives and how we think about and handle money and possessions" (9).

While I conceded that there is indeed a connection between the two, I doubted it was fundamental, so I was eager to read on to see how he would support it. Much to my surprise, Alcorn supports his big claim, and convincingly so. But he does much more; he makes a biblically sound case for generous giving founded on what he calls, *The Treasure Principle*: "You can't take it with you—but you can send it on ahead" (18).

Unearthed From Scripture

With theological carefulness and economy of words, Alcorn invites readers to accompany him on a thoughtful journey as he explores what Scripture teaches about giving. At the outset, he unearths *The Treasure Principle*, which he argues is the biblically-grounded reason for generous giving.

Along the way he identifies six Treasure Principle Keys, which are biblically-shaped attitudes which motivate generous giving. These keys are concisely crafted, and they give evidence that Alcorn has studied long and hard about what God's Word has to say about the topic. He provides transparent biblical support for his conclusions, allowing readers to hold them up to the light of Scripture to see if they are indeed so supported.

Illustrated Through Testimonies

Alcorn illustrates the message of *The Treasure Principle* through his own movie-like testimony of how the Lord used a difficult circumstance to lead him and his wife on a journey to become joyful, generous givers. He goes on to illustrate it through numerous testimonies of other people, of extraordinary and ordinary financial means, who also discovered the joy of generous giving. And he convincingly dispels the false idea that one needs to be rich in order to be generous.

Indeed, as Alcorn points out, the Macedonian believers in 2 Corinthians 8, who were very poor, are an ongoing illustration of joyful generosity, despite their poverty. Thus, all readers, whatever their financial circumstances, will be inspired and envisioned by one or more of the testimonies.

Focused on Eternity

Among the most commendable features of *The Treasure Principle* is Alcorn's consistent reminder of the eternal consequences involved in how we view and handle money and possessions. He soberly observes: "He who lays up treasures on earth spends his life backing away from his treasures. To him death is loss" (45). Conversely, he points out: "He who lays up treasures in heaven looks forward to eternity; he's moving daily towards his treasures. To him death is gain" (45). Readers can't help but thoughtfully evaluate where their treasures are, and whether death will mean loss or gain.

If you have not read *The Treasure Principle*, hopefully by now you are wondering exactly what the six Treasure Principle Keys are. Read the book for yourself. Blessing awaits.

6

SERVING WITHOUT SINKING

By JOHN HINDLEY

Matt Chapman

Senior Pastor, Grace Church Bristol (Bristol, United Kingdom)

The Shaping Virtue of Servanthood

IF YOU EVER FEEL like your joy in serving is dwindling, perhaps especially as your life and ministry grow in busyness and complexity, this book offers sweet refreshment for the weary, serving soul. John Hindley's *Serving Without Sinking* is richly rooted in Scripture throughout its pages and helpfully autobiographical in places as well.

As Hindley shares in his introduction:

> Christian service shouldn't leave us feeling irritated, exhausted, guilty, proud, bitter or lazy—but all too often I chat to Christians who feel one (or all!) of those things. I see them in myself, too ... This book comes out of what had happened in my soul, that turned serving Jesus from

the thing I enjoyed the most into a chore that I resented and a duty I had to fulfill (8).

It's that honesty and openness from the author that makes his content so relatable and easy to engage. Hindley skillfully and graciously describes that growing weariness in us that we don't readily recognize in ourselves, but which is often lurking in the shadows of our service nonetheless.

Serving Without Sinking is a simple book but by no means simplistic. It addresses a whole variety of reasons, across its thirteen short chapters, as to why our joy in service might gradually give way to bitterness or burnout. Perhaps service has become mere duty, or instead we've turned it into our very life and identity. Perhaps we've been serving to make other people notice us, or even to impress God himself and gain his approval of us. At root, Hindley shows how joyless service almost always stems from a wrong view of Jesus, or ourselves, or other people.

What I found most helpful was that after identifying the common signs of a sinking servant, Hindley swiftly redirects our gaze to the reality that it's not our service that most matters anyway; it's Christ's. "[He] came not to be served but to serve (us!) and to give His life as a ransom for many" (Mark 10:45). So our lives are not fundamentally built on how we serve him, but on his all-sufficient, saving service toward us.

It's this reminder, Hindley says, that frees us first and foremost simply to enjoy and bask in his love. Only then will we find ourselves newly "set free to serve him longer, harder, braver, truer than we ever could otherwise" (10). Jesus offers his followers a "restful yoke" (15). "Rest from needing to achieve, to succeed, to be noticed, to be the best. Not rest from serving, but rest in serving (119).

This is a book that will not only encourage pastors, but one that could be placed enthusiastically into the hands of every serving church member and believer. Nor is its focus limited to only serving in the church, but also in the home, the workplace, and amongst family, neighbors, friends and strangers as well. It's full of Christ and full of grace, and the relief and good counsel it offers is impressive given its small size.

Perhaps the best recommendation I can give is simply one of personal testimony. This book refreshed my weary heart to press on in joyful service and in happy dependence on the Savior who came not to be served, but to seek, serve, and save, by gladly laying down his own life for us.

7

THE HOLE IN OUR HOLINESS: FILLING THE GAP BETWEEN GOSPEL PASSION AND THE PURSUIT OF GODLINESS

By KEVIN DEYOUNG

Erik Rangel

Pastor, Legacy Church (Yuma, AZ)

The Shaping Virtue of Godliness

ONE CAN SCARCELY BE in, around, or even aware of the church very long without deriving some notion of "holiness." Clearly, there is God's perfect holiness, and then there is some effect that his holiness is to have on his people. Beyond this, and despite our Bibles, there has developed a confusion even among gospel-loving people—a confusion leading to dangerous error.

The result is what DeYoung calls a "hole" in our view of and growth in holiness.

His diagnosis is plain from the title and subtitle of the book. What ensues is a thoroughly biblical, often humorous, and altogether hope-filled encouragement toward true holiness for all the right reasons.

A False Dilemma and the Lie of a "Safer Danger"

DeYoung describes views of the gospel and of holiness that have led many in the church to run from legalism, right past holiness, and into a dangerous carelessness. He observes,

> We know legalism (salvation by law keeping) and antinomianism (salvation without the need for law keeping) are both wrong, but antinomianism feels like a much safer danger (19).

The good news is that errors from either extreme are not our only options. Scripture makes clear that sin is what God has saved us from, holiness is what God has saved us to.

> For the grace of God has appeared, bringing salvation for all people, training us to renounce ungodliness and worldly passions, and to live self-controlled, upright, and godly lives in the present age (Titus 2:11–13).

Sorting out Mandates and Motives

In remarkably succinct terms, God's strong commands are shown to flow from his rich grace. Rejecting any hint of salvation being by works, or that sanctification depends solely upon us, DeYoung points to the many scriptures calling for holiness, listing more than three dozen biblical motivations for pursuing holy lives. Again, the clarity and brevity on such a complex topic are exceedingly helpful and what we've come to expect from the author.

In Defense of Effort

DeYoung blesses the reader by putting in its right place the role of human effort toward holiness. He identifies constant striving toward holiness as the command of Scripture as well as the glad response of the saint.

In very pastoral tones, the author writes,

> There is a gap between our love for the gospel and our love for godliness. This must change. It's not pietism, legalism, or fundamentalism to take holiness seriously. It's the way of all those who have been called to a holy calling by a holy God (21).

Holiness, Already and Not Yet

Lest the believer ever feel the pursuit of holiness is futile, the author stirs our anticipation of ongoing increments of holiness until the perfect comes. DeYoung gently meets the reader in acknowledging present indwelling sin, yet he encourages the Christian toward the Spirit-enabled joy of increasingly pleasing our Lord on our way home to him.

Elaborating upon the Westminster Confession of Faith, DeYoung writes, "God not only works obedience in us by his grace, it's also by his grace that our imperfect obedience is acceptable in his sight" (68).

Dishonorable Mention – Sexual Immorality

While the book is a broad overview of the Bible's teaching on the holiness of believers, one chapter is dedicated to a particular fault besetting the church today—sexual immorality. By the end of this chapter and its special emphasis, the reader can only be glad it was included. We have slipped. A timely word indeed.

A Strong Nudge Toward a Deeper Dive

Relative to the subject matter, this is a very brief book. Even so, it makes a compelling biblical case for holiness as it cites hundreds of Scriptures and other works to move the reader toward continued examination. Including indices, short chapters, and a very thoughtful set of study questions, DeYoung gives the believer a true toolbox for ongoing personal and/or group study.

The Hole in Our Holiness provides real help in celebrating the saving and sanctifying grace of God.

Made in the USA
Middletown, DE
20 October 2022